THE

CONSEQUENCE

OF

CHOICE

My Inside Voice

By Bernard R. Pilgrim

The Consequence of Choice: My Inside Voice
by Bernard R. Pilgrim

Library of Congress Control Number: 2022917290

ISBN: 979-8-9868444-1-1 (Paperback)
ISBN: 979-8-9868444-0-4 (eBook)

Published by SOURSOP PRESS LLC
Cover design: Premade Cover Design

For more information and bookings, visit www.soursoppress.com.
Mail to: P.O. Box 813, Bronx, New York, USA 10469

Dedication

To my wife of twenty-six years, who told me to stop moving my lips when I'm thinking or talking to myself in public. She doesn't want anyone to think she's married to a crazy person. Therefore, I learned to use my inside voice.

Table of Contents

Preface

I came to New York in 1999, and it took me a while to adapt to my new, ever-changing reality: a melting pot of cultures with a vast array of unwritten rules to navigate carefully and patiently, in order to avoid offending anyone's racial, religious, sexual, or cultural sensitivities. Additionally, over the years, this bombardment of social issues has forced society to confront its inner demons in meaningful ways.

Within the framework of relationships, two topics have become an ever-present concern and source of confusion for me: The muddying of the waters associated with women's rights—that they shouldn't have to beg for, but instead, return as reparations for past societal injustices—and the new, uncharted, and undefined roles women now must play in their relationships and marriages.

Stop!

Yes, I used the word role, which is an ugly word filled with negative connotations, because religious and cultural institutions have aided in the perversion of this principle by creating a hierarchy within the framework of gender-specific responsibilities. This uncertainty has left men and women meandering in a state of ambiguity in their quest for equality and love. However, genuine equality has always been about the division of labor and shared responsibilities based on natural and learned skill sets.

This precarious circumstance of undefined roles has given rise to a manifestation of identity loss in terms of individual responsibility within relationships. Some women who assertively argue for total relationship equality still find themselves perplexed by their desire for romance and what that entails.

However, others still expect men to provide the same benefits of the conventional male role:

- Opening doors
- Asking women out on dates
- Paying for dinner
- The giving of romantic gifts
- Requesting marriage
- Being protectors and providers

Unfortunately, some men have become confused because their natural proclivities are no longer acceptable but falsely interpreted as misogynistic and sexist.

The weird reality of women wanting conventional principles from men is wholly and straightforwardly counterintuitive. Why should men still play or honor a traditional role or purpose within their relationships or marriages if society believes having a gender-specific role is a form of oppression and inequality?

To understand this difficulty, I realized that abandoning labor distribution within relationships and marriages, rather than fighting for equality, has created an identity loss that's fracturing the very essence of our relationships. I later interpreted this rift as a gray area between men and women. The realization that this gray area exists, along with an understanding of the pain and confusion it has caused, became the stimulus that drove my inner thoughts and self-dialogue to the point where I desperately needed to find answers to this puzzle.

I've never seen women as subservient, weak, or less-than, but I noticed that men worldwide had two distinctive, pervasive relationship practices. They treated women as necessary, valued partners within their relationships, knowing that their every action, as husbands or fathers, if not self-scrutinized, could cause irreversible physical, mental, or emotional damage that would affect their wives' and children's lives. This acknowledgment, however, isn't sexist in any way; it grants men the ultimate, respectful way to perceive women as potential wives and future mothers of their children, along with an understanding that they must respect the unique differences between men and women. Additionally, on the other side of that belief, some men still believe they should lead and control all aspects of their relationship, and women should be subservient, listen, and obey.

So, in my quest to anatomize this gray area, I separated and examined the unwritten ways some men and women now view one another.

- Men as habitual cheaters, liars, little boys with commitment phobias, deadbeat fathers, and good-for-nothing sons of bitches who think they're God's sexual gift to women.

- Women as one-night stands, friends with benefits, whores, sluts, or placement holders until they find someone more appealing or sexually attractive.

As the picture of this gray area became clearer through the discovery of each puzzle piece, it led me to a profound yet simple conclusion: The Consequence of Choice is the catalyst that has spawned the current turmoil between men and women.

Acknowledgment

I am grateful to my family, friends, and work colleagues who graciously allowed me to peer into their personal lives over the years and discuss their relationship successes, failures, and complex issues.

Introduction

Over the years, I've grown frustrated with the stupid answers society has concocted for why some men cannot be faithful or lack the aptitude to commit. Sadly, some women have readily accepted and parroted those same false narratives as doctrines of truth to justify the dismissal of men's bad behavior or as antagonistic weapons of condemnation against men.

In this book, I unlatch the doors to my inner thoughts and my self-dialog regarding the unvetted choices and responses I've witnessed that both men and women continue to make regarding their dating and relationship tendencies, which were influenced by their past traumas, financial desires, misplaced ambitions, fear, desperation, learned misguided sexual attraction, values, morals, and the lack of self-discipline.

The symptoms of any illness often indicate that we need medical attention. Our doctor gives a prognosis and prescribes the essential medications to make us whole. During those periods of our physical illnesses, have we ever stopped to ask the following:

- What was the origin of the disease?
- When did it jump from animals to humans?

- What group of people was responsible for the spread of the infection?

- How many people died?

- What was the response of the Church and the government?

- Who discovered the cure?

And why? Because none of those things matter to us. All we want is to heal in the here and now—and truthfully, it shouldn't or doesn't matter.

"Those who cannot remember the past are condemned to repeat it" (Santayana, 1905).

Therefore, if the history of our physical illnesses doesn't matter to us, only the symptoms, why do we blatantly ignore the signs of bad relationships or marriages, arrogantly bathing in self-pity and the memories of traumas, and refuse to seek professional help for our psychological issues?

Let's put things in perspective here. History can only tell us how we got here, but we're the ones who must learn from past mistakes and triumphs. Hopefully, we can find the answers to improve our lives and overcome our struggles. We blame our history of bad relationships and everyone else for our problems, yet, just like Zombies or the Walking

Dead, we move from relationship to relationship, spreading our infectious, emotional sickness like it's no big deal, and in our wake is a trail of toxicity and shattered lives.

On my journey, I witnessed how men's and women's interpretations of relationship issues drastically differ and how those distorted conclusions have led to decisions that have caused so much mental and emotional ambivalence.

To properly analyze those interpreted contradictions, I considered the past and present cultural changes in societies' courting, dating, and marital habits by looking at some of the norms and principles that govern human relationship behavior, including, whether correctly or not, the abandonment of conventional tenets has done us a disservice, as this means we don't understand and can't even consider the pearls of wisdom that those relationship principles were supposed to impart. Many of today's new relationship principles and norms have greatly benefited our society. In contrast, others have contributed to the dismantling of family structures and the erosion of moral tenets such as love, honor, fidelity, and commitment.

This abandonment of morals has led us to an extreme place where we ferociously try to fulfill our emotional voids by surrendering to our primal nature, quenching our physical and sexual desires, regardless of who gets hurt.

This undisciplined sexual appetite is the unruly stimulus that has allowed some men to ignore their place within their relationships. In some women, this same behavior has forced them to believe their superficial beauty is the only source of their value and sexual attraction.

In this book, I look at the negative and positive results of today's romantic complications that affect our relationships and how today's hostile relationship environment likes to blame, condemn, or point its fingers, arrogantly ignoring its contribution to the failure of relationships based on feelings, while simultaneously being void of little to no facts.

Throughout our discussion, we'll take a unique approach by examining the choices some women have made and continue to make, along with their rationale for those decisions, through their eyes. We will also explore what they hoped to achieve by examining the romantic ideologies that some modern women have adopted. We'll then discuss how men have interpreted and responded to women's romantic choices and whether men's actions or behaviors are inherent traits.

Examining interrelationship issues through women's perspectives and reading men's responses may seem strange, unorthodox, and even offensive. Initially, you may think I'm critical of women's decisions. To that, let me say no. Given today's adverse romantic relationship outcomes, I suggest that some women deeply analyze their relationship choices and the desires of their hearts, so that facts, rather than emotions, inform all their decisions. Stop! I never said women's judgments are indifferent. I noted that some women might need to analyze their romantic decisions so that men can accurately interpret the messages in their choices. And, in doing so, they may achieve the goals they genuinely desire and long for, such as true love and fidelity.

We'll also consider what I call a great hidden truth, ripped from society's consciousness. That principle is that men's responsibility isn't to lead in their relationships; it's to serve.

I know what I just said goes against everything you were taught or led to believe. So, before you become irate and condemn me on social media as some heretic or unorthodox thinker, I'll explain this contradiction in the chapter 'The Training of Men,' specifically in the subheading 'The Paradox of Leadership and Servitude,' related to the consequences of choice.

Those who linger or wallow too long in the memories of past traumas often ignore the need to heal their present reality.

(Bernard R. Pilgrim)

Chapter 1

Why Do Men Cheat?

That's the question.

A s I sit here contemplating this complex difficulty, I've been replaying unbridled conversations
I've had with male friends and acquaintances, who, in most
cases, would never share their innermost feelings openly.

I've also thought about my in-depth discussions with
women while replaying their social interactions with their
significant intimate partners and other men. All the relationship articles I've read, and the many shows I've watched,
have led me to conclude that most women in our society believe all men cheat.

I apologize for my curiosity as I inquire about your thoughts and opinions on this matter.

Your response may fit with today's accepted views on this matter:

- Men are horny dogs.

- They're addicted to sex.

- They have no self-control.

- They think they're God's sexual gift to all women.

- They can't keep their dicks in their pants.

- They think they'll somehow be sexually missing out if they commit to one woman.

- Men are just assholes and bastards, good-for-nothing sons of bitches who need to die, die, nasty, horrible deaths. Ouch!

However, I believe there's one valid fundamental reason some men cheat. Unfortunately, many in society question whether it is a man's natural propensity to be monogamous. Let's call that belief for what it is—bullshit. This seductive theory is just a copout by men who want to be promiscuous and women who desire a man by any means possible.

Before answering the question, "Why do men cheat?" let's establish a baseline of indisputable facts. The bedrock of our judicial system establishes what's permissible and what's not, setting the framework to protect our societal freedoms. Disregarding the rule of law means we would be in non-compliance, committing a crime, or engaging in an impermissible act. We, as individuals, are our own judicial system in the same way. We're the ones who must give or grant consent to others concerning what we consider permissible and not permissible in our lives. I'm not talking about the indifference that stems from the actions of others regarding the decisions they make toward us; I'm talking about the things we control and what we allow others to do to us.

What Is Consent?

- "Permission for something to happen or an agreement to do something" ("Consent," n.d.).

What Is Rape?

- "Unlawful sexual activity, most often involving sexual intercourse, against the victim's will through force or the threat of force or with an individual in-

3

capable of giving legal consent because of minor status, mental illness, mental deficiency, intoxication, unconsciousness, or deception" ("Rape," 2022).

What Is Force?

- "To make someone do something difficult, unpleasant, or unusual, especially by threatening or not offering the possibility of choice" ("Force," 1995).

What Is Sexual Harassment?

- According to the US Equal Employment Opportunity Commission, sexual harassment is a form of sex discrimination that violates Title VII of the Civil Rights Act of 1964: "Unwelcome sexual advances, requests for sexual favors, and other verbal or physical conduct of a sexual nature constitute sexual harassment when submission to or rejection of this conduct explicitly or implicitly affects an individual's employment, unreasonably interferes with an individual's work performance, or creates an intimidating, hostile, or offensive work environment" (US Equal Employment Opportunity Commission, 1964).

The exploitive action of rape being an unlawful sexual act against a person's will, whereas unwelcome sexual advances, requests for sexual favors, or physical conduct of a sexual nature constitute sexual harassment, which is a non-consenting act; we must accept that the power of our consent regarding the people we allow in our beds, our lives, and with whom we choose to love, honor, and commit is our choice and responsibility.

The undeniable fact is we're the ones who must grant consent, and this also encapsulates another indisputable truth: the principle that it's a woman's body and her choice regarding all the decisions she makes concerning it, such as the following:

- Who she sexually gets involved with is her choice.

- To vet or not to vet her romantic partners is her choice.

- Whom she chooses to be the father of her offspring is her choice.

- Whether she chooses to protect herself against unplanned, unwanted, and out-of-wedlock pregnancies by using birth control or contraception is her choice.

- To have or not to have an abortion is also her choice. I'm not basing this on religious morality, but rather on subjective morality.

Some of us may not accept these facts as accurate; nevertheless, let's continue discussing our relationship difficulties.

However, the question remains, "Why do men cheat?"

The facts that guide my convictions may seem downright offensive or hurtful because they challenge and contradict what we've been taught or accepted as truths about relationships. Please understand these are just the findings I discovered as I plunged into the relationship turmoil and behavioral patterns of men and women. To this, let me say "sorry," and I'm afraid this is where I might offend, but the reason men cheat is – you.

"Wait, what in the hell did you say? Just another typical man, blaming women for all the nonsense men do."

No, I'm not blaming women for the irresponsible personal failures of men and all the dreadful misdeeds they do; I said you're the reason men cheat. So, if you don't mind, please let me clarify that statement as one of the truths I've come to accept about relationships. You may not realize this, but you're the ones who continually set your relationships up for failure by repeatedly making the same unvetted choice. You habitually do it without hesitation. I've often wanted to hold my head and scream, "What are you doing?" or "What were you thinking?"

You may not want to listen to my lamentations because they go against everything you believe. It sounds like some masculine insensitivity or a betrayal of your self-esteem, especially from a man.

So, before we go any further, there's one word I want you to remember: *choice*.

Some women believe men only want to sleep with as many women as possible, with no commitment. Have you ever considered the other side of that statement? Suppose a man is sleeping with twenty women; you're also declaring that twenty women are giving themselves to this man, along with the sexual pleasures of their bodies?

"Yeah, but he might be lying to all those women."

That's true, but whose fault is that? Isn't it the responsibility of those twenty women to vet, discover, or figure out his intentions toward them before they let him into their beds?

Let's take everything we've discussed and their elucidations regarding choice, consent, rape, and force. Then we must conclude that if a man can only have sex with a woman with her permission or license, the question becomes, who's having sex with whom? And no! I didn't stutter; let me repeat that question based on the facts we've discussed within the relationship truths framework. If men need your permission to engage in sexual activity with you, are men running around having sex with women?

Or is it women who are running around having sex with men?

Please, please answer the question.

And if you don't want to, then let me respond with complete clarity of mind.

- Women are the ones who control access to sex.
- Men can only make a request or beg for sex and affection.
- Women are the ones who must give consent to men for them to jump into their beds, which is a woman's unquestionable choice.
- Women are the ones who emotionally cultivate and decide which physical attributes and moral standards they'll allow themselves to find sexually attractive in men.

Therefore, because the power of choice is yours, and you control access to sex, we must conclude and accept that it's women who have been running around having sex with men, and not men who have been freely having sex with women.

Finally, another fundamental relationship truth is out there, an ah-ha moment that needs to sink in—Men aren't the ones having sex with women; women are freely having sex with men.

The Power of Choice

The power of whom you let into your life, your children's lives, and your bed has been and will always be yours. You have allowed the desperation of "wanting a man, got to have a man" to cloud your perception.

Look, I'm not naïve or ignorant to the reality that there have been many times throughout history when wars, cultural malfeasants, false religious doctrine, political motivations, and the atrocities of slavery have tried to appropriate women's power to control their bodies, and the right to choose one's sexual partners and husbands has caused a scourge of devastation that continues to vibrate worldwide.

Juliana Menasce Horowitz and Janell Fetterolf (2020), with the Pew Research Center, reported on worldwide optimism about the future of gender equality: "Across thirty-four countries surveyed, a median of ninety-four percent think it's essential for women in their country to have the same rights as men, with seventy-four percent saying this is very important."

This continuing growing acceptance reflects the efforts of past generations of women who fought, died, and won many of the rights modern women enjoy today, including the right to be who and what they want to be, determine who they could love, marry, and allow into their bed, and have control of their bodies.

The power of choice should always be the God-given right of every woman, and it should be paramount to those who have fought, won, or made significant strides in the struggle to fight alongside those who don't have a political voice or equal civil rights.

You keep consenting and allowing the dogs, the users, the abusers, the cheaters, the liars, and all the other stupid-ass men into your lives and your beds. And when those relationships end, you then turn and blame the dogs, the liars, the cheaters, and the abusers for all the problems and failures in your relationships, and not the choices you've made.

When I stated earlier that you are why men cheat, I based it on the fact that, if you keep habitually choosing to get involved with cheaters, and they cheat or are unfaithful in all aspects of the relationship, whose fault do you think it is? I know you don't want to hear this because the truth often hurts sometimes, but it's your lack of responsibility for not properly vetting the men you let into your beds.

Many people don't consider the significance of their choices or actions; we constantly operate in an emotional state where we don't think before we act. However, having as much information as possible before making any decision is crucial for rationalizing our thoughts and desires, which helps us minimize the negative aspects of our choices.

I truly believe and will defend the rights of all women to do the following:

- Dress any way they want to dress
- Talk and express themselves in any way they want to
- Act in any manner they deem fit without apology
- Freely have sex with anyone they want to
- Be any and everything they want to be and go anywhere they want to go

However, we're discussing the consequence of choice, which we have no control over, whether good or bad. For example, you can run in Central Park at 3:00 a.m. to clear your mind and embrace the joy of carefree living.

Unfortunately, you may fail to recognize or even consider that someone else, that same morning of your spiritual cleansing run, also made a conscious decision that they want to either rob, rape, or murder someone.

Their actions will become the consequence of the word I asked you to memorize–choice.

Unvetted Choices

We're responsible for all the choices we make and the possible outcomes that follow. We shouldn't blame anyone else for our failures. As I noted, if we choose a cheater, and they cheat, can you blame the cheater for cheating? How can we blame a dog for being a dog when he starts doing what all dogs naturally do?

The reactions of others to our choices are their responsibility and their choice. However, when you choose to get involved with a cheater you didn't correctly vet, and he cheats, that issue is your tribulation to bear.

A man's propensity for cheating is his burden and responsibility to correct and manage; it's not yours. Trying to fix others' perceived flaws is a futile endeavor.

Women's Intuition

You've stated there's something called a woman's intuition. Let me ask you a few questions:

- How is it that your woman's intuition gets conveniently pushed to the side and only seems to reappear when your relationships aren't going the way you've orchestrated?

And why is your woman's intuition now communicating its desire to seek answers to the questions you should have gotten from your lovers at the beginning of your entanglements?

- Are you in a relationship?

- Are you dating anyone else? (There's a difference, so let me explain).

A woman will ask a man, "Do you have a girlfriend?" And, when he says no, they'll conclude he said he was single and not sexually involved with anyone. However, he may be dating ten women who think he's in a relationship with each of them because they're sexually involved. Nevertheless, he may not consider his dating or sexual practices as relationships, and the truth is, dating is not a relationship.

- Are you married?
- Do you have kids?
- Do you pay child support?
- Can I meet your children, family, and friends?
- Are you sexually involved with your children's mothers?
- Do you believe in the institution of marriage?
- Do you think sex and love are the same thing?
- What's your stance on fidelity and commitment?
- What are your intentions for the future?

Acquiring the answers to these questions at this late stage, when you're already sexually involved, could derail or destroy your present relationship reality, causing immeasurable hurt and pain. But do you realize you keep placing yourself in these predicaments by becoming emotionally and sexually invested in your relationships before appropriately vetting your potential lovers?

You need to ask yourself the following:

- Why do you keep ignoring all the red flags and your gut feelings at the beginning of your relationships?

- Why do you push your family's and friends' opinions aside, labeling them jealous, or trying to control and destroy your happiness?

- What's so wrong with taking the time to authenticate your potential lover's stated intentions toward you or finding out their moral and value structures at the inception of the relationship before you allow them into your bed?

Chapter 2

The Miseducation of Sexual Freedom

O ver the years, women have often fought and died for what they believed was their God-given rights:

- To be free from oppression

- To pursue purpose and plot new destinies

- To be in control of their bodies

- To decide whom, they could love and marry

- To vote and to receive equal pay

- To have access to health care, including reproductive rights

- To be protected against sexual harassment

At some point during the quest for those liberties, some women started to believe that part of being in control of their bodies and their sexual freedom meant having the right to participate in what they perceived as men's sexually illicit promiscuity. This perception was not entirely their fault; instead, it was a result of wars, politics, economics, and changes in norms, spirituality, and cultural beliefs. However, sexually acting like men is a fallacy, a misconception, a misguided delusion, and a false narrative.

"Well, if men can sleep around, we can do it too."

Sexual Truth

This misguided belief unintentionally introduced a cultural change into society, turning courting, dating, sex, and relationships into a game or a sport. This is where all the conflicts lie within the spectrum of relationship confusion — the gray area.

If you ask any man who's had thirty sexual partners how many women he has been with sexually, he'll tell you that number or even more.

However, if you ask a woman that same question, in most cases, she'll say,

"I've only slept with three guys; I'm not a whore."

Women claim that if men can do it, they can too. Yet they hide the truth about their sexual liaisons because they're either ashamed, don't want people to view them as promiscuous, or don't want to suffer the painful feeling of being slut shamed. Maybe that awful feeling is their conscience, spirit, or woman's intuition.

The Cost

Women say they want men with sexual experience to pleasure them in bed. But, like everything else, it comes at a cost, and it's that emotional cost many women are not prepared to pay. With the acceptance of the false narrative of having the right to act like men sexually, women inadvertently gave up their influential power and ability to guide men to see them as more than sexually desired creatures.

This transgression unwittingly opened the floodgates, allowing men to have casual sexual encounters with as many consenting women as humanly possible. Unfortunately, this newfound pleasurable reality led men down a path that transformed their nature into a ravenous, unquenched, sexually promiscuous corruption that has profoundly deceived men into no longer associating sex with love, fidelity, or commitment.

"But I still don't want a man who can't sexually please me, and I don't have the time or patience to teach a man how to."

Sexual Experience

Please do me the honor of enlightening me about how a man becomes excellent sexually.

What! You don't know?

Then let me humbly inform you about how a man becomes excellent in bed sexually. It's through practice, the habitual act of having sex repeatedly with as many willing partners as humanly possible.

I know you may not want to hear this, or it may seem overly real to you, but men become great at sex by having sex with as many willing partners as possible.

For some strange reason, you believe the men who rock your world sexually, who've been habitually sleeping around with multiple women, will miraculously change and stop being promiscuous and become faithful and committed to you because you've developed intimate feelings. You've allowed your romantic delusion to convince you they're the ones you've been waiting for, your soul mate, your knight in shining armor. Seriously, what the hell?

Love, Fidelity, and Commitment

Here's a gospel of relationship truth that no one may have ever told you: Love, fidelity, commitment, values, and morals aren't biologically, spiritually, or mechanically engineered.

These characteristics are behavioral traits acquired through observing family values and norms, which become firmly established within a person's mental construct through continued practice within a family structure.

You, however, have been falsely led to believe that when you engage in an intimate sexual relationship, your partner automatically becomes faithful and committed to you. This false doctrine is a lie from the pit of all that is unholy.

When a man or woman needs more discipline in how to honor and practice the principles of love, honor, respect, and fidelity throughout their lives, they will be incapable of celebrating their love for you by being faithful and committed in a relationship or marriage. They may give you the shirt off their back or even their last dollar, but they will still find themselves sleeping around with other people.

"But why?"

I'm glad you asked.

Learned Behavior

The environments they grew up in never taught them how to connect the dots of associating sex with love, sex with fidelity, or sex with commitment within relationships. They're habitually doing the things they identify with and have done throughout all their past and present relationships.

These individuals will never be faithful to you; they'll continually cheat because they were led astray from that path long ago, which connected love, fidelity, commitment, and sex. However, the lack of those values in your partner's life isn't why your relationships have failed; it's not even the fact that their infidelities ruin your relationships. Once again, it's you.

"What the hell? How is this our fault, too?"

You're the ones who keep choosing not to vet the men you share your lives with and the men you allow to enjoy the sweet nectar of your bodies.

What was that word I asked you to remember?

Oh yeah, choice!

Chapter 3

The Sport of Sex and Dating

Y ou need to understand that men don't play sports or games with any emotional attachment. Men often view sports or games as battles they'll fight with rage, aggression, and a reckless, dogmatic abandonment of self-preservation, which leaves them devoid of sympathy for their opponents.

Unfortunately, this lack of attachment in some men can lead them to unconsciously venture into the realm of hate and uncontrollable anger, which can produce an abusive permissive dispensation, leading them to become mentally and physically abusive toward their relationship partners. This disassociation is why some men can have numerous sexual affairs or liaisons with multiple women and walk away without emotional or psychological attachment.

When society allowed dating to turn into a competitive sport, men adopted a sexual animalistic nature, voiding them of their naturally positive response toward women, aided by the conscious decision of women to act like men sexually.

Unfortunately, men started treating women like men, as enemy combatants, with only one goal: to win sexually at every encounter. Now we're reaping the consequences of those actions; an unseen wound society has left unchecked and festering—the destruction of relationships and marriages.

Men don't care about other men's feelings and emotions; they tease each other until it intensely hurts. Have you ever watched a boxing match where the animosity between the fighters is palpable, and it appears they're trying to kill each other with every punch?

However, as soon as the fight ends, all the hostility and anger subside; they hug each other, show concern, and move on like nothing ever happened. That's because it wasn't about any emotional attachment; it was all about aggression and passion, the pride and joy of winning.

Traditionally, the masculine nature compels men to fight, hunt, and kill, and to refocus quickly for the next battle. This emotional abandonment is why men and women often struggle to play sports together effectively. Instinctively, men will try to crush their opponents at all costs; they may change their aggressive tactics if their opponents are women, but eventually, they'll do the same things they do to their male counterparts. So, what makes you think you'll ever win in this sport of sex and dating against men?

You'll sexually and emotionally lose every single time, without fail. You may think you're winning because you've been benefitting financially or because you're the one who ends the relationship, but that's not winning. The men you've slept with are now a permanent sexual fixture in the fabric of your mental and emotional construct as they casually move on to their next sexual conquest.

The strategic way men play this sport of sex and dating is to have as many sexual encounters as possible without emotional attachments, relationship labels, or commitments. In most cases, men don't even know they're playing the game. They have somehow been taught that their behavior is their birthright and who they are, yet they're unaware that their conduct is a deception that has become an accepted truth.

Men learned long ago and continue to be taught by the reaffirming actions and the messages by some women within society that women are only attracted to men for what they possess and not for who they are.

Some women consider men's inner characteristics, such as kindness, patience, and financial responsibility, to be weak, cheap, and dull. So, men, aware of this fact, have accepted that having glamorous materialistic objects like wealth, fame, and power will attract women like moths to a flame; thus, they proudly and boastfully use these tools to achieve their sexual goals.

You need to understand that men will help you pay your bills or even take care of all your financial needs as long as they can have sex with you on their terms. Their financial or romantic gifts don't signify they love or care about you or will claim you as theirs; it's just part of the sport of sex and dating.

Too often, women find themselves in a delusional state where they believe they're in relationships with a certain caliber of men; however, in the sport of sex and dating, they're being used sexually. This outlook may seem misogynistic, but you need to take your blinders off to this reality. You have been playing this game of sex and dating by using your superficial beauty and the promise of sexual pleasure to achieve your idealistic romantic relationship goals, but, honestly, how has this sexual game worked out for you so far?

- You've amassed lots of dates and one-night stands that led nowhere.

- You've wasted years in long-term, dead-end relationships.

- There's no indication there will be a future engagement or marriage proposal.

- You're constantly in and out of meaningless relationships because you desperately don't want to be alone.

- You've had unplanned, unwanted, out-of-wedlock pregnancies.

- You've been forced to decide whether to have an abortion or give a child up for adoption.

- You've raised fatherless children or experienced the mental anguish of not knowing who your children's biological fathers are.

- You're always depressed and dreadfully encumbered with internal guilt, the embarrassment of allowing yourself to be sexually used, and forced into carrying that heavy pain of regret into each new relationship.

- You're engaging in or being trapped in transactional relationships to maintain a lifestyle beyond your financial capability.

- You're older and still trying to compete with younger, more attractive women, and feeling emotional bitterness, leading to the arrogant thoughts of "I don't need a man; I'm an independent woman; men can't handle me."

Should I go on?

Or maybe I'm being a bit presumptuous.

You're probably getting everything you desire. You may even think the passion between you and your lover is love. However, what you're undoubtedly experiencing is just the natural rhythm and dance of the game.

Chapter 4

Directed Perception

The ability of a woman to command a man's desires toward her true essence.

For men to have a positive response toward you, one that sees you as their future wife and the future mother of their children, you must direct their perception of you. The power of directed perception only existed in the realm of women; it is and should still be a part of a woman's intelligent design, one that deserves to be taught, guarded, and protected.

This protective power, which should have never been relinquished and foolishly abandoned by women, created a misguided power shift that allowed it to be captured in the dominion of men. Regrettably, this imbalance gave men the power to redefine women and the unilateral aptitude to determine the type of romantic relationships they wanted. Nonetheless, men should never be allowed to redefine you due to the following:

- Their own sexual, fictitious, superficial realities
- The false narratives of others
- Your unrealistic manufactured representation of who you are, which stems from your imprudent behavior and unwise choices

Your ability to direct potential partners to see you for who you genuinely are should come from the following:

- The recognition that your superficial beauty is and should reflect your inner qualities and strength, your true essence, the everlasting beauty that will not fade with time
- The acknowledgment of your natural and acquired skill sets as a woman and a life-giver

Your inner qualities should create a line of demarcation that forces men to assess whether they possess the necessary qualities and strengths to seek an audience with you.

This line of distinction will allow men to feel confident yet vulnerable in their approach, knowing they'll have to face judgment about whether they will be considered worthy of your love, joy, and happiness. They'll contemplate whether they're praiseworthy of embracing your true beauty and caressing your sensual bodies by demonstrating they possess the mental and emotional maturity to see you as wives, future mothers of their children, and equal partners in marriage. Once again, a man's interpretation of you should be orchestrated and guided by the display of your standards, values, and self-worth, and not your well-formed ass and voluptuous breasts.

Natural Instincts

The sport of sex and dating has impaired and corrupted the morals of some men, forcing them to perceive women as follows:

- Bitches and whores
- One-night stands
- Side chicks
- Possible friends with benefits or placement holders
- Sexual playthings to use as objects of masturbation

This false perception is the catalyst that drives some men's illicit, sexual, uninhibited passions. A man's natural impulses and abilities will always lead him to analyze, interpret, and draw conclusions based on what he sees, hears, smells, touches, and tastes. For these reasons, men were great in their traditional roles as hunters, protectors, and warriors. Their instincts enabled them to process environmental cues, allowing for instant life-or-death decisions.

Your romantic signals and how you sexually present yourselves to men as potential companions are the relationship's environmental cues. Therefore, men will perceive, interpret, and pursue you based on their inherited internal processing. That is why your directed perception is of utmost importance in determining positive or negative results; you may think this isn't right, it's sexist or even misogynistic, but that's the way it has always been from the dawn of time and always will be. And the more you and the forces in society fight to change men's natural inclinations, the more they'll stay the same.

Men will instinctively internalize and pronounce their judgment regarding the person they perceive you to be, based on the following:

- The way you walk, your posture
- The way you talk, your subjects of conversation

31

- How you dress and accentuate your physical appearance (whether you think it's fair or not has nothing to do with you wearing the latest fashions or designer clothes.)
- The way you interact with people and your attitudes
- The way you treat your loved ones, family, and friends
- Your ethics and the standards you set and continually observe

And once men judge you based on those things, that judgment will stand and never change:

- If he sees you as a whore, you'll always be a whore.
- If he sees you as a one-night stand, you'll always be just a one-night stand.
- If he sees you as a side chick, you'll always be a side chick.
- If he sees you as just a friend with sexual benefits, you'll always be a friend with sexual benefits.
- If he sees you as a placement holder or his long-term girlfriend, you'll always be his long-term girlfriend, a sexual companion, and nothing more.

However, if he envisions you as his future wife from the first time he lays eyes on you, that changes everything.

The Shopping Habits of Men

When a man desires to purchase a car, he does his due diligence by educating himself about the value and worth of the vehicles within his price range; then he meticulously seeks the right one. We can all agree that most men hate running from store to store, so once they've found what they're looking for, especially if it's on sale, they'll purchase it without hesitation. Most men won't procrastinate and foolishly let someone else notice the value and worth of the car they want to buy, thereby granting them the opportunity to own it. In the same way, when a man meets a woman with virtue, value, substance, and self-worth, it will immediately compel him to do whatever it takes to make her his wife as soon as possible.

And why, you ask?

Because he understands that, if he procrastinates, other men will recognize her true intrinsic qualities and attempt to make her their ultimate prize, or that one day, she might wake up and realize she could do so much better than him if she wanted to.

We just discussed the following:

- How the sport of sex and dating has changed men

- The responsibility of women is to direct men to see their values and standards

- Men's relationship shopping habits, and how a woman's intrinsic qualities will compel a man, as if God ordained it, to make her his wife without hesitation.

Long-Term Relationships

How often have you witnessed men and women who've been in long-term relationships and preached they don't believe in marriage; their relationships end, and they're both married to other people six months later?

Ladies, I regret to inform you that I don't believe in long-term dating relationships.

I think it's a lie that people tell themselves when they've decided to settle, play the long game in the hope of marriage, or pretend to commit while repudiating the very essence of legal commitment.

"Wait a minute; I've been in a long-term successful relationship, thank you very much."

Yes, we all know couples who've been together for twenty or thirty years; nevertheless, we also know marriage isn't just about companionship, which we'll discuss later.

However, the questions that perplex my mind concerning what you consent to and the person you claim to love are based on the following:

- What else is there to learn or discover about you for your lover to consider marriage?

- Why do you continue to accept the illusion of relationship tranquility, year after year, despite being in a long-term relationship?

- Why hasn't he found you worthy of possessing the qualities that allow him to express his love by legally committing to you in marriage?

- Why are you only good enough for sex, having his children, and being a warm body at night, and not worthy of marriage?

- How do you not recognize that his noncommitment and dereliction of duty to you as a woman is vulgar, disrespectful, and denigrating because he thinks so little of you?

- Aren't you tired of being his placeholder, his assured sexual pleasure, while he habitually cheats?

- Why are you allowing your fear of being alone to hold you in relationships like a hostage, being his milk without him owning the damn cow?

Don't you think you deserve more? Seriously, what the hell is wrong with you? Or maybe you believe you don't have any value or self-worth, so you'll take what little you can get.

Well, I think you do, and if no one has ever told you this before, then let me be the first to say it: You have value and worth, regardless of whatever happened in your past.

To succeed in college, you must graduate and receive your degree. The opposite is also true: if you don't graduate or earn your degree, you haven't been successful in college. If you seek employment at a business looking to hire someone with a college degree and demand employment because you believe you were successful at college but didn't graduate, and don't possess any official documentation to prove it, your application will be rejected.

A successful relationship means you have graduated to marriage and maintain the legal documentation of real commitment, which lets you know, with confidence, that the person you love has found you worthy of being legally theirs.

Chapter 5

Killing Weakness

D o you realize that, in the animal kingdom, the females select the healthiest superior males who have proven their strength and ability to reproduce through combat, the extravagance of their bright colors, or their seductive, choreographed dance moves to mate with and to be the biological father of their offspring?

They know male weakness must never be allowed to breed if their bloodline is to survive. No form of liability in the animal kingdom is permitted, and, in most cases, predators kill off those who are old, sick, wounded, or abandoned. Although harsh, these actions or practices help preserve the health and viability of many species.

So, ladies, why do you keep sacrificing your love, joy, and happiness by giving access to your wombs and the sexual pleasures of your body like cheap merchandise to weak-ass men who aren't worthy of you and woefully incapable of being your husbands and the responsible fathers of your children?

Why do you keep casting your pearls before swine?

"Do not give dogs what is sacred; do not throw your pearls to pigs. If you do, they may trample them under their feet, and turn and tear you to pieces" (*New International Version*, Matthew 7:6).

Remember that word, choice?

Chapter 6

The Real You and The Scale of Beauty

S uppose you let yourself be comfortable in your skin and give men the chance to see and experience the real you. Not your representative or the superficial person you've been pretending to be, but the authentic you who's charming, sweet, kind, and quirky but proud of who you are, warts and all. Then, you'll establish and position yourself to attract the correct type of man who wants and appreciates a woman just like you.

Here's something you may have found offensive or considered sexist: the golden scale of beauty (phi) or the attractiveness scale (one to ten) that the beauty industry has used to judge a woman's level of beauty, which has caused substantial psychological damage, pain, and depression in women through body image shaming. I suggest you take a different approach to these mathematical scales of beauty by adopting a different perspective.

The standard of beauty that has been portrayed in the media over the years through brilliant marketing has forced women into believing they can all be ten on the scale of beauty if they purchase manufactured beauty products and are willing to physically transform themselves into the industry's image of attractiveness, the goddess of fashion and beauty. However, have you noticed that today's fashion and beauty standards have led women in their respective societies or with different cultural backgrounds to act, dress, and even physically appear the same?

Look at your Instagram, Twitter, TikTok, or Facebook accounts, or take a walk down the street and see for yourself.

In consenting to the industry standard of physical beauty, women have unconsciously altered their personalities to match their new mentally perceived image and newfound status as tens. That innocent, kind, sweet, quirky girl you are somehow gets lost amid all that confusion, inner turmoil, and struggle.

The dire consequences of your fantasy of pretending to be an industry ten, including your newly adopted personality shift, have led you to attract the wrong kind of men into your life. The physically gifted, fast-money, famous men who in the past wouldn't have given you the time of day are now standing at your doorstep because you have been deceptively and arrogantly propagating the life of a ten.

Now, blinded by your new pretend ten status and delusional sexual desirability, your inflated ego, and your social media picture-perfect fame, you don't realize you lack the necessary skill set to operate in that new world.

Your dreams of romantic relationship grandeur have now stopped you from being attracted to the type of men who would have gladly committed to you.

Carelessly, you have unwittingly allowed those without good intentions, the habitual liars, cheaters, users, and abusers, through the doors and beyond the protected walls of your heart, whose actions may cause considerable mental anguish, derail your future, or leave you permanently emotionally scarred for the rest of your life.

Being unapologetically proud about displaying your values and self-worth and staying true to yourself as the sweet, kind, quirky girl—warts and all—is better, even if society may consider you a three, four, or five on the artificial beauty scale. Then you'll attract the correct type of men who have been praying and hoping to find a girl like you, men who will see you as tens, as their wives, and the future mothers of their children.

So please get this through your thick skulls: you are, have always been, and will always be a ten to the appropriately devoted men who fall madly in love with you and will be forever captivated by your everlasting beauty. And be proud and honored to give you the gift of commitment.

You don't need to become that stupid, imprudent, artificial ten that the beauty industry wants you to become, just for them to sell you their beauty products and endless weight loss schemes.

Suppose you stay faithful and love the person you are, warts and all. Given societal realities, I assure you the right types of men will find you. Just like the females in the animal kingdom we discussed earlier, you'll find yourself with multiple suitors vying for your attention.

Chapter 7

The Bait and Switch

Today, based on the marketed image of the beauty industry, women have unconsciously asked men to forsake being attracted to who they are and sexually crave the
embodiment of beauty they desire to be. However, as I have
mentioned before, you need to direct a man's perception of
you. So, please understand that, whether you believe in or
reject this stated principle, your active participation or unconscious inaction will still require a man's discernment,
and his interpretation of you won't change once it is in-
grained in his psyche. You may not realize that when you
fictitiously become someone else, and men become physically and emotionally attracted to your representative, that
attraction will not change.

Men are mentally and emotionally incapable of that metamorphosis; they may sincerely try to, but it will always fail because of the deceitfulness of finally meeting the real you, even if the relationship is already sexual. Unmistakably, this deception becomes the reason some men aggressively dump women. These are some of the same men and women falsely labeled as dogs, users, and no good sons-of-bitches, without taking any personal accountability for the confusion they caused. Why should men be deceived and fall prey to the bait-and-switch game some women play?

"What about men? They play games too!"

The difference is men deceive women about what they possess—or their profession—not their physical appearance; that's what we're talking about here.

Some women have consciously decided to accept the false relationship doctrine that men should only be attracted to their superficial beauty and not to who they are. Therefore, men should ignore the following:

- Your hair and nails aren't that long.

- You're not that tall.

- Your lips aren't that plump.

- Your breasts and butts aren't that voluptuous.

- Your eyes aren't the color they appear to be.

- You may not be as fit and healthy as you think. And most of all, you have kids.

When men are only attracted to your superficial beauty and not to who you are, it will always be a physical, sexual attraction and nothing more.

How can you rationalize and expect men to fall in love with the real you after you've deceived them into being sexually attracted to the person you've been pretending to be?

Seriously! How can you be so arrogant as to expect and demand this metamorphosis from men?

This delusional state of mind is a self-manufactured misfortune. If you genuinely want love or a relationship that leads to a great future, then you need to understand that when a man falls in love, he needs to fall in love with the real you, warts and all, and nothing will subvert his perception of you. Also, his desire and attraction toward you won't change or fade with time.

Chapter 8

Superficial Beauty

Have you ever watched any of those reality shows like *Four Weddings*?

If you have, you would have noticed most of the women on those shows aren't runway models. They're just ordinary-looking women of all shapes and sizes, adorned with what society may view as beauty imperfections.

It would be best if you recognized what lay beyond their superficial beauty.

Most of these women were found or acknowledged as their future husbands to have value, virtue, and substance —the intangible internal attributes that men find most intriguing, beautiful, sexy, and alluring—the true, unfading beauty of a woman that keeps men captivated.

I want you to consider the reality that some of the most gorgeous and sexiest women in the world, especially those in the entertainment industry, somehow can't keep a man or find themselves constantly cheated on or divorced.

So, how has your superficial beauty worked out in getting and keeping a man with all of today's beauty enhancements?

- Has it brought you great joy and the happiness you believe you deserve?

- Has it bestowed upon you deep love and fidelity?

- How about marriage?

- Has it stopped your sexual partners from cheating on you?

- Has it stopped you from being just a one-night stand?

- Has it prevented men from using your bodies only for their sexual fantasies, and desiring nothing else?

- Has it stopped you from being abused?

- Has it erased the pain from your past failed relationships?

Seriously, with all the investment of time and money into your outward appearance, which you often consider your most important asset, your pride and joy, how has it worked out so far?

The endeavor to only cater to outer beauty, whether you want to believe it or not, declares to all men that they should only be attracted to your body and all the sexual pleasures your erotic body will bring.

A Good Man

I've often heard some women declare, "I want a good man," but what is a good man?

- Is he supposed to mend your broken heart and erase all the hurt and pain left from your past?

- Is he the one who indulges in all your insecurities by not hanging out with his friends and not speaking to or looking at other women while allowing you to check his phone and social media accounts constantly?

- Is he supposed to listen to your complaints, read your mind, and know exactly when to help and when not to fix things?

- Is he the one who caters to your romantic and emotional needs, fulfilling whatever you request?

- Is he the one who lets you take out your frustrations in fits of rage and anger by allowing himself to be mentally, emotionally, and physically abused because you think it's your right as a woman to do so?

- Is he the one because he's a bad boy, is well-endowed, sexually experienced, and capable of pleasuring you?

- Is he the one because he's wealthy or has a specific career that can financially support you and your kids in the lifestyle you believe you deserve?

Is this the kind of person you consider a good man?

How do you not see that everything we just listed concerning your idea of a good man was about your selfish desires and had nothing to do with who he is or his qualities, morals, and family values?

Unquestionably, everything was all about you.

- A good man stands on his own two feet and takes pride in being financially accountable, but isn't too proud to ask for help.

- He's sexually responsible and acknowledges his reproductive rights and responsibilities by not putting himself or his sexual partners in the position of having unplanned, unwanted, and out-of-wedlock children or abortions.

- He believes the institution of marriage is the legal covering and protection for his future family.

- He humbly defines himself through his morals and values, as well as the practice of fidelity, honor, love, and commitment throughout his life.

- He aspires and sets financial goals for himself and his possible future.

- He lives a life of joyful servitude, finding purpose in honoring the things he's committed to, which may be his job, his family, an idea, or even a deity. He does this with the understanding that, if he doesn't have someone or something greater than himself to serve, he'll zealously worship his selfish, sordid desires.

Indulge me for a moment and consider this before you go on your next journey or quest to find a good man. I want you to take the time to contemplate the question I believe every woman should ask themselves: "Why should a good man desire you?" I know this question may perplex because every woman thinks she's a good woman and that it's her job to find a good man from among all the dogs. Yet the question remains, "Why should a good man want you?"

Before you answer this question, let's start by taking a few things off the table:

- Your physical beauty and sex appeal
- Your sexual aptitudes, how good and excellent you think you are in bed
- Your job, career, or business—because they aren't determining factors most men contemplate when attracted to a woman

And why should we do this?

Because hundreds of other women are much prettier, sexier, and vastly more proficient in bed than you, men can even pay for beauty and great sex if they want to.

So, with those things in mind, let me ask you that question again,

"Why should a good man want you?"

And, by the way, that same good man you believe you're entitled to runs his own company, has a career, owns a house and a car, has investments, retirement savings, and extra funds for travel, and doesn't need anyone to provide for or help him build his life.

I'm not trying to be arrogant or insensitive by repeating the same question. I'm just trying to inspire you to focus on what you should be contemplating and the questions you should be asking yourself:

- What do I have to offer a good man besides my physical attributes?

- In this era of equality, can I equally build a financially stable future with a good man, or will I be his financial liability?

- What about my virtue or my reputation? Do I have the morals and values needed to build the kind of family he wants and needs, or am I morally bankrupt?

- Am I mentally and emotionally healed and rehabilitated from the traumas of my past relationships?

- Or am I willfully carrying around emotional damage, longing for someone to lay my burdens upon, hoping they'll bring me the joy and happiness I need?

- Am I an agreeable woman who can allow someone else to lead?

- Do I possess the capability of submitting to a good man, whose success is due to his discipline and hard

work, and who will need me to be his asset and not a
burden?

- What behavioral traits have I been displaying that
  have attracted certain men to me?

- What characteristic flaws have I allowed myself to
  become sexually attracted to in men that may have
  contributed to all the failed relationships in my life?

- What must I do to inspire good men to truly see me,
  the real me, my true internal beauty? That will spark
  love's eternal flame within their souls by creating an
  emotional and spiritual deep desire, triggering a
  yearning within their hearts to envision themselves
  not living one more day alone in this world without
  me.

That being the case, without your good looks and the
promise of sexual pleasure, what else are you bringing to the
relationship table that necessitates good men to acknowledge
you? What attributes or essential qualities do you possess
that will persuade an excellent man to find you worthy of his
love, fidelity, honor, commitment, and financial protection?
Remember, we're talking about the kind of good men you
desire.

Squandered Beauty

Over the years, I've seen many drop-dead gorgeous women spend most of their youth or sexually attractive years running from relationship to relationship and reaping the benefits their superficial beauty brought them. They've had romantic dates, dinners, weekend getaways, flowers, expensive shoes, clothing, jewelry, makeup, financial support, and whatever else their romantic heart desire—only to wake up to the reality that they're older, confused, and baffled because the type of men their youthful beauty attracted aren't captivated by them anymore. Yet they remain arrogantly incapable of freeing themselves from the trap of covetousness, and all the things that brought them temporary joy and shallow happiness, which are now at war with their need for love, companionship, trust, honor, fidelity, and commitment, have now risen to reclaim their rightful place in their lives. Unaware that this resurrection of needs is the catalyst for their internal confusion, they self-medicate their emotional infirmity by trying to recapture the glory of past superficial exploits, unintentionally opening the doors to their toxic state of mind.

- **Anger:** Believing all men are dogs, liars, and cheaters

- **Age-inappropriate dressing:** I know this is a sensitive subject because the fashion industry has led society to believe that fashion is ageless

  Yes, I know, "Off with my head."

- **Cosmetic surgeries:** Competing against the eventuality of time and younger women

- **Desperation:** Finding any man capable of financially supporting them

- **Guilt:** Haunted by mistakes and missed opportunities for real love

- **Hatred:** Blaming men for their current position

- **Jealousy:** The tearing down of other women for their self-gratification

- **Being sexually indiscriminate:** Having multiple sexual partners, even if they're married

These women failed to recognize that their beauty was a gift and should have been used to attract the right kind of men, those who wanted to build a life with them based on love, fidelity, commitment, and principles. However, they unconsciously used their beauty to attract the kind of men they wanted to prey upon, manipulating them into giving them all the worldly things their hearts desired. Regrettably, they utterly failed to comprehend that they weren't predators; they were the prey used by men to fulfill their carnal appetites.

Faced with the harsh reality that the type of men they wanted no longer desired them, they desperately throw themselves at the kind of men they once rejected, only to discover that those once-scorned men, who are older and wiser, don't want women like them anymore.

Every Good Man Deserves a Good Woman

In every relationship, there will come a time when your outward beauty becomes ordinary to your partner, and the sex becomes just sex. That doesn't mean he stops seeing you as beautiful or doesn't enjoy having sex with you; it just means he's now looking beyond those things and seeing all of you, the real you, and your intrinsic qualities. That will command the center stage of your life and become the erotic acquisitiveness he finds most alluring and will keep him interested in you and the relationship forever.

The question then becomes—what mental, emotional, and spiritual substance can you provide to feed your good man's heart, soul, and mind when your beauty and sex aren't all he needs? And what moral virtues are you displaying to let him know you'll be the kind of mother he wants for his children?

A good man may believe he's in love with you; nevertheless, he realizes your physical beauty and erotic pleasures have captivated and trapped him because you made him feel you needed him to save and rescue you.

Subsequently, when he finally figures out the person you're pretending to be isn't the kind of woman he needs or desires, he's left with no choice but to make the agonizing decision to walk away from you and the relationship.

Please understand that, if you don't contribute any substance to your relationship other than beauty and sex, you're not an equal, loving partner but a parasite. Eventually, you'll do what all parasites do to their host.

You've probably been finding good men, but have allowed your selfish, parasitic behavior to impair your judgment, so that you were the one destroying your relationships.

You may need to ask yourself, "Who was the common denominator in your failed relationships?" And that answer, once again, is you.

Chapter 9

Parasitic Apathy of Relationships

M any individuals don't realize they're in parasitic relationships, based on their partners' behavioral patterns within the context of their relationships. My observations have led me to conclude that a desperate, misguided desire to be wanted or needed, or the anguish of not feeling loved, can emotionally lead us into these dangerous entanglements. Therefore, we often fail to recognize our own behavior or our partner's flaws as red flags, indicating that we're either hosts or parasites in our relationships. Some of these red flags are as follows:

- Cheating

- Disagreeableness

- Financial irresponsibility

- Lying

- Neglect

- An addictive nature

- Being unsympathetic

- Shamelessness

Relationship parasites only care about one thing: the fulfillment of their mental, emotional, sexual, and financial desires while duplicitously caring little or nothing about the life of their hosts. Unfortunately, what we may consider or believe to be deep-rooted, intimate love may instead be the intense, carnivorous feeding frenzy nature of our parasitic partners, unsympathetically sucking us dry. Therefore, when we become emotionally or financially depleted, our parasitic lovers move on to their next vulnerable victim, leaving us weak, heartbroken, and filled with regret and the possibility of us becoming parasites in our subsequent relationships. Unaware of the infestation, the relationship host slowly withers from their partner's consumption of their natural re-sources, creating a painful void, an insatiable hunger, and an unquenchable thirst that forces them to seek sustenance else-where to replenish their mental and physical needs. Society then falsely pronounces judgment and brands the hosts as cheaters, without realizing the hosts are the victims of para-sitic relationship abuse and that their parasitic partners are the ones who caused the infection in the first place, which led to the host's infidelity. And, yes, I'm arguing the indi-viduals who cheat in their relationships may be the victims, not the immoral perpetrators.

"Yes, I know. Off with my head."

I'm asking you to consider that, in the same way, just as you don't condemn or victim-shame the mentally and physically abused, you shouldn't blame the victims of para-sitic relationship abuse either. And you shouldn't brand them as cheaters, dogs, or bitches when their infidelity is a self-treatment in response to the abuse they have suffered.

This parasitic relationship abuse syndrome is why some people, hosts, or parasites jump from relationship to relationship.

Parasites will claim they want a good man or a good woman, but they don't; they're looking for the perfect target to exploit—someone with either a superhero complex or an "I'm helpless, please save me" mentality. Their uncompro-mising mission is to manipulate and deceive their host by any means necessary, by unconsciously and psychologically tricking themselves or their lovers into believing that what they have together is true love. This deception is maintained by frequently minimizing their lover's efforts in fulfilling their romantic aspirations as inadequate, forcing them to do better.

The Host-Parasite

Then there are those (the hosts) who desperately desire love, or what they believe is true love. Unfortunately, their internal desperation leads them astray, causing them to unconsciously seek out potential lovers, whom they feel need rescuing (the parasites). This false path leads the host to think that their actions of generosity will prompt their partners (the parasites) to give them what they desperately crave—loyalty and love. Unfortunately, in their passionate quest to fulfill their desires, they fail to recognize that guilt-bought loyalty and love only temporarily feed their internal obsessions, which turn into an addiction and an infestation of a parasitic partner, ravenously devouring them spiritually, emotionally, and financially.

Regrettably, we fail to comprehend that this permissible psychological addiction of being wanted or needed forces us to exploit others to fulfill our selfish desires, which unintentionally impairs our morality.

Our unchecked appetites become the stimulus that drives our sexual and emotional attraction to those who can become the hosts or parasites within our relationships.

We constantly complain about our parasitic lovers' or hosts' unhealthy behaviors, but we never leave.

We bathe in the pleasures of being satisfied; we swim in the ecstasy of being wanted and needed. We delight in the drama of being unfulfilled, used, or abused—the highs and the lows of constant discontent—only to find ourselves being pushed straight into the arms of someone else to fulfill our desires or replenish our depleted inner strengths.

Financial Abuse and Traditional Roles

One of the character flaws or traits of a relationship parasite is financial abuse.

Let me be clear: no cultural belief, religious doctrine, or legal basis exists for a man or woman to be coerced into financially supporting their lover within a relationship. The only exceptions are spouses, children, and parents. Also, in the case of cohabitation, if you decide to muddy the waters outside the bonds of marriage in a common-law relationship, then that's your financial problem to work out.

Your relationship partner is not your father, mother, or guardian. It's not their responsibility to financially support you within a relationship. But let's get back to the topic at hand.

Some women don't believe in adhering to traditional societal or romantic roles. Understandably, it's modern times, and women can do well for themselves; they genuinely don't need any man financially. Yet others still believe it's a man's responsibility to care for them financially. They may not say it because it's not politically correct, but it's a requirement. Suppose you genuinely want equality of the sexes. In that case, men shouldn't be forced into, or expected to play, any traditional roles in their relationships or families, just like modern women do, and, frankly, why should they?

You can't have it both ways. I'm not saying women can't pay their bills, but having the extra finances helps some women live the materialistic lifestyle they desire beyond their financial means.

Society has subverted the correct belief that men should take care of their wives and children into the false doctrine that it's a man's responsibility to provide for every woman in every relationship.

This ideology has hurt the ability of both men and women to build wealth for their future families. There's also an emerging ideology that has begun to gain traction among some women: the notion of 'dating down.' In other words, why should women have to date men who make less than they do financially?

The problem with that statement is that men have been "dating down" for generations without complaint. Stop! And let me acknowledge what you just said aloud.

"Men didn't let women work."

However, historically speaking, is that political narrative accurate?

- In the past, families' wealth was built through farming, hunting, fishing, and labor division. Procreation was the earliest method used to expand the family business's labor force. So, what part of that history suggests men didn't want women to work?

- During the classical era (600 B.C – 476 A.D), the Middle Ages (476 A.D – 1450 A.D), and the early modern period (1450 A.D – 1750 A.D), when nations went to war, hundreds of thousands of men died on battlefields to protect their countries, lands, and families. Who did all the work of providing for and protecting their families when men didn't return home?

What part of that history suggests men didn't allow women to work?

- Between 1800 and 1878, when 65 percent of the land surface was under European empires (colonialism), were men the only ones working while their wives stayed home? What part of that history suggests that?

- Maybe it was during the start of the new world, Black slavery in 1502, American slavery from 1619 until the 13th amendment of 1865, the Civil War (1861–1865), Reconstruction (1865–1877), or Jim Crow (1865–1968)? What part of American history suggests men of color or their enslavers didn't want women, especially Black women, to work?

But I digress.

The irony is that those women who are angry about dating down still want men who make more money than they do, which suggests a desire for financial security.

I guess the words of John Batiste Alphonse Karr (1848), a French critic, journalist, and novelist, still reverberate: "The more things change, the more things stay the same." ("Alphonse Karr," 2020).

Traditional religions and some cultures believe a man should leave his father and mother and cleave to his wife (*New International Version*, Matthew 19:5).

Ephesians 5:28 (*New International Version*) states, "In the same way, husbands ought to love their wives as their bodies. He who loves his wife loves himself."

Let me reiterate my earlier statement: a man's financial responsibility is toward his wife and family, not his girlfriend. I'm not talking about child support; every man should financially support his out-of-wedlock children, period.

Single women should be economically responsible for themselves, act like adults, and not rely on men or relationships for financial support. Why should a good man consider you a good woman if you're financially irresponsible by living above your means?

Suppose you earn only $500 but live a $1,000-per-week lifestyle. Where are you getting that extra $500 per week if you don't have a trust fund, an inheritance, or a family member supporting you?

The problem is that those funds must come from somewhere, and if you're not earning it on your own legally, then someone else is giving it to you. A good man will have to consider this reality and realize that, if he gets involved with you, he might be the one who'll have to fulfill that role of maintaining your desired financial lifestyle.

Please understand, I'm trying to get you to comprehend that, if you're financially irresponsible with your money, how can a good man, whom you want, trust you with his?

Remember what I said earlier: financial irresponsibility is a trait of a relationship parasite.

The false relationship doctrine that it's a man's responsibility to provide for women financially has deceived men into becoming financially irresponsible in dating or being in a relationship. Men now spend their money on women's hair, nails, clothing, shoes, flowers, cosmetic surgeries, expensive dates, and weekend getaways.

How are men supposed to have a prosperous financial future, fulfill their dreams, lead a life filled with purpose or meaning, build a home, get married, and have children if the women they date misappropriate their financial wealth and resources for their own selfish romantic gratification?

Maybe I'm wrong, quite naive, or you don't give a damn. After all, it's just men, not your financial problem, so why should you care?

Parasitic Prostitution

Using a relationship as a cover for financial gain is another form of abuse or parasitic prostitution. And, in many cases, it has become an adopted but false, learned behavior that society regurgitates. This type of relationship is like standing on a street corner or being a high-priced call girl or gigolo. The only difference is that those individuals on street corners, as well as the high-priced call girls and gigolos, are the only ones who aren't lying to themselves about who they are.

If you believe a good man is financially responsible and plans for his future, then you should question your edict about calling yourself a good woman if you aren't doing the same.

The problem of financially relying on someone else puts you in a compromising position where you could un-willingly become subservient or even potentially exposed to the harsh reality of abuse. It may even ferociously drive you to control your partner's life so you can keep living beyond your means.

Parasitic prostitution also means relationships are never about financial equality, respect, and honor. There-fore, it leads both the host and parasite to unconsciously give into their partner's ever-changing mental, emotional, and sexual demands, believing what they have together is true love. I'm not saying couples shouldn't help each other out, but to what end?

Why should anyone be forced into investing their financial resources in every relationship without guarantees?

I've heard women often say, "I don't want a man who's broke." And if I may quote:

- **The late Gwen Guthrie (1986):** "No romance without finance" ("Aint Nothin Going On," 2023).

- **Destiny's Child (1999):** "Can you pay my bills?" ("Writing's on the Wall," 2023).

- **TLC (1999):** "No Scrubs" ("FanMail," 2023).

Average-earning men trying to compete in today's dating market find themselves broke, dumped, or pushed to the side after being used and abused by parasitic women. These are the same types of men some women don't seem to want today. They include the plumber, the electrician, the carpenter, the sanitation worker, the bus driver, or the guys who work in construction, just because they don't have a six-figure salary to give them the fairy-tale Hollywood lifestyle they believe they deserve.

A Bigger Picture

Suppose you're fortunate to be one of those women who are a significant part of your partner's financial responsibilities. Have you ever considered using those financial resources to create a business that could put you, your partner, or your children in a much better, more prosperous economic position instead of spending it to fulfill your selfish desires?

Throughout history, women have utilized the naturally acquired skill sets passed down from mothers to daughters to create building materials, garments, food supplies, and medicines from what they could gather, grow, or hunt. Unfortunately, some women were forced to disregard those skill sets in many cultures due to the following:

- Constant belittlement or the negative, degrading stereotypes uttered by other women in the higher echelons of society
- Conditions of colonialism and slavery
- Innovative convenience of manufactured goods and services

- Censure by political ultra-feminist groups who saw those skill sets as a continued dissent, the perpetuation of being domesticated, and a hindrance to women's progress

Suppose you want a decent designer dress. You may have to pay hundreds of dollars for it. A meal at a restaurant, or simply ordering in, might cost you between twenty and forty dollars. So-called domesticated women, traditional wives, or your grandmothers would have bought groceries and cooked several meals that would have fed their families for a few days, or purchased fabrics and made four or five dresses. Please consider all the money those so-called domesticated women have saved over the years by using their skills to produce the things they needed.

How amazing do you think your partner would feel knowing you took what they gave you and turned it into some form of wealth that could financially benefit both of you, now and in the future? That way, you're no longer a financial liability but a financial asset, on your way to a relationship based on genuine equality.

Oh yeah, Choice.

Chapter 10

Dating/Relationship Misconceptions

L et's look at some relationship misconceptions some women seem to believe and have even regurgitated among themselves as the gospel of relationship truth:

- Love, fidelity, commitment, and sex are instantly connected manifestations.

- Communication only means discussing what you want and what your partner has and hasn't done.

- Acknowledging your partner's thoughts or concerns, or even trying to grasp their emotional messages from their actions or reactions, is irrelevant.

- Your partner should know how you're feeling and what's on your mind, even though you haven't told him.

- A man expressing his emotions is weak and unattractive.

- It's a woman's right to fix or change a man; if she can control all aspects of his life, he'll be faithful.

- A man must satisfy a woman's mental, emotional, physical, and financial needs.

- A man should shoulder the burdens of a woman's past failed relationships.

- Men are selfish and only think about themselves and their sexual gratification.

- A man who honors his work and responsibilities and is financially acute is somehow dull.

- A man living at home with his mother is a mummy's boy.

- In this age of equality, it's okay for women to abuse men mentally, emotionally, and physically. Unfortunately, some men lack honor or a moral code and will act similarly.

- Men should still be duty-bound to play traditional roles within their relationships, but women shouldn't.

- Men shouldn't have any emotions, no discernment of a connection, or awareness of loss regarding a fetus when a woman desires to have an abortion because it's her body and her choice.

- When a woman has a miscarriage or natural abortion, their significant other is somehow required to express their emotions by having a sense of loss by showing empathy for her and the death of their child, even though men have been indoctrinated and instructed through the legal system to accept that it's a fetus, not a child.

- When some women state they want a tall, handsome, fit, and financially secure man, society considers those qualities as women's standards, and they shouldn't settle for less.

- When men proclaim they want beautiful, physically fit, not promiscuous, and childless women, they're told their mentality is wholly sexist and misogynistic; men should accept women for who they are.

Where did these illogical, flawed relationship doctrines come from, and how have these false ideologies worked out so far?

Vetting

Look at your past hookups and relationships, and ask yourself, did you properly vet any of your lovers before you got sexually involved?

- Did you meet their family to determine how they treated one another?

- Did you inquire about their learned value structure?

- Did you ask whether they associated sex with love, sex with fidelity, or sex with commitment?

- Did you meet any of their friends? As the saying goes, birds of a feather flock together (Baldwin, 2020).

- Did you ask any of them or try to find out if they were dating, in a relationship, or casually having sex with anyone else?

- Did you take them around to meet your family and friends so they could help you determine if any red flags were missing?

I'm sure you didn't, due to the fear of losing them because of what some of your untrustworthy girlfriends might have done or said, or the harsh, unrelenting questions your family members would have asked to protect your mental-emotional state, physical health, and future.

- Did you intelligibly communicate your principles to any of your past lovers?

- Did you give them the time to grasp that having your love and your body required a consistent demonstrative promise of fidelity, with a future vision of commitment?

- Did you give them the time to unlearn their misconceptions about relationships and reflect on their unhealthy choices and actions in past relationships, thereby granting them the opportunity to learn how to love and appreciate you correctly?

- Did you give them the time to assimilate that love and sex are two different entities, that they can operate independently, and that sex is not an expression of love?

No, I somehow don't think you did. And why? You didn't want to be alone, or maybe you just wanted sex, a warm bed at night, or someone to take care of you and your kids, emotionally or financially.

The Baby with The Bathwater

Let's now look at some past dating and family relationship principles that today's society has disregarded and come to perceive as oppressive, degrading, and an assault on women's civil liberties.

- That there should be defined roles within marriage
- The vetting of the daughter's potential suitors to see whether their morals, beliefs, and intentions were compatible, aligned, and truthful
- That girl's parents had the right to disregard all disadvantageous suitors to protect their daughter's virtue and reputation while guarding her against poor romantic choices
- That sex should be reserved for marriage

Societies should have analyzed and studied past relationship principles for their intended good. However, modern society disregarded them as if they were rubbish from a forgotten age, and in that indifference, relationships began to suffer. The false shared belief that women were the weaker vessels was heinous and oppressive. That biased, false doctrine of religions, cultures, and politically systemic practices inflicted considerable mental and emotional pain, which aided in the deterioration of the upward mobility of women into the higher echelons of society, especially among women of color.

To achieve and protect the ideology of equality and women's rights, women, in their zeal to right the wrongs of society's misguided past, hastily discarded the relationship principles of the past. Unfortunately, they also purged themselves of all the purposeful effects those principles had bestowed.

Those initially developed belief structures and the benefits they afford weren't in place because society thought women were weak or less than men. Different cultures put those written and unwritten principles in place for one thing and one thing only:

- The discipline of men. Yes, you heard me right—a bridle to control the wild sexual impulses of men.

"Don't throw the baby out with the bath water."
(Murner, 1512)

Chapter 11

The Discipline of Men

Women say chivalry is dead; that's because you killed it.

"I know, I know, off with his head."

Let's take a different approach to this controversial subject.

Chivalry among men evolved as a natural response to how women valued, presented, and epitomized themselves by humbly displaying their values and self-worth to the world. This allowed men to see them as precious creatures, a prize worthy of their protection, respect, honor, and commitment. The gallantry of chivalry offered a window—a front-row seat — into the souls of men, revealing how they saw or felt about women. Men, led by a sense of politeness and gentility, willingly and without fear expressed their deep emotions through acts of kindness and appreciation toward women. Opening doors and giving up their seats or positions prioritized a woman's safety and security over their own comfort.

But chivalry wasn't about you, even though you reaped the benefits of it. It was about the training of men to evolve into seeing you not just as sexual beings to be conquered but as potential wives and cherished, equal members of society, which allowed men to have that correct, positive response toward women previously discussed.

However, men's perspectives changed once organizations decided men's considerations toward women were unequal treatment, a sign of feminine weakness, and sexism.

Men require laws, principles, and a disciplined structure to channel their natural capabilities and aggression constructively, benefiting their families, villages, and communities. Men need to operate in a structured environment that forces them to habitually repeat the same process to become better, stronger, faster, and more proficient at whatever skill set they want to perfect.

This process of self-discipline directly relates to what I mentioned earlier, so please forgive me for sounding like a broken record. Love, fidelity, commitment, and gratitude are habitually learned behaviors and are not automatic.

Demanding them from men you haven't vetted will always be an impossible or fictitious dream; it's like trying to get water from a damn rock.

Some women believe they can't raise their sons to be men; this is an absolute lie from the pits of all that is unholy. For thousands of years, mothers understood their role in laying a foundation that imprinted their family's morals and values into their sons' hearts and minds so that, when they came of age to be instructed by their fathers, they would be able to see women as the following:

- As mothers, daughters, wives, and fortresses of love, kindness, comfort, and peace, and worthy of their love, honor, and the utmost respect and dignity.

- As the most valued commodity within their village, as equal partners and providers, capable of managing every aspect of their family's lives..

Chapter 12

The Training of Men

War has always been considered the province of men, and it wasn't in any way a sexist view. It was in response to the positive perception of men toward women: to protect those they loved —the village's most valuable commodity—you.

Men valued the lives of their wives and children above their own and did that with an instinctive, brutal, focused aggression, unleashed at the very sight of any danger. Men would willingly run into battle, knowing that their loved ones' protection and safety were more important than their own lives and well-being.

To usher their sons into manhood, the village men would take the young boys when they came of age, strip away their childish behaviors and any psychological damage inflicted by their mothers, and build a disciplined structure on the foundations already laid by the boy's mothers. This new structure provided the guidelines to navigate the importance of their future role as men.

The Paradox of Leadership and Servitude

The justification for the lives of men isn't leadership. Their purpose is to serve those they love: their wives, children, extended families, communities, and environments. And, in that state of servitude, being dutiful toward their responsibilities, men find their strength and purpose, which is their leadership role.

This servitude encapsulates the leadership of men, too:

- Protect their promise of fidelity and commitment to their wives and children against all who would do them harm, such as the attention of other women
- Protect their family's mental and emotional sanity and stability, allowing love, joy, and happiness to be an ever-present reality

- Protect the relationship's economic environment, which enables them and their wives to provide for their families. True equality

Male leadership is interpreted today simply as embodying the role of financial provider, and all other leadership roles or guidance from men in relationships are met with appalling hostility.

However, men's natural abilities and mindset need to be dogmatically focused through discipline so they can become the leaders they were born to be. Men need a vision or a cause, a deity or an individual, and a family or an organization to serve. And without a purpose, men will worship their selfish sexual desires without emotional attachments.

This emotional disregard is why it becomes essential for men and their sons to have a healthy, optimistic view of you. Without it, men will continue to see you as sexual prey.

Sex, The Province of Marriage

"Why should men see you as worthy of marriage if you willingly give your milk away for free?"

In today's secular society, the idea of no sex before marriage is considered an antiquated religious belief, a form of oppression, a weapon used effectively against women to control their bodies and imprison their sexual desires in the framework of marriage. Unfortunately, the initial principle of sex reserved for marriage was misinterpreted and passed down as truth. But it was never meant to control women by forcing them to accept being told whom they could or couldn't have sex with or even whom they should marry. This principle was for the discipline of men and not women; it was for harnessing the sexual appetites of men, which can quickly grow out of control if women become promiscuous.

Societal leaders believed that, without sex as one of the benefits of marriage, men would uninhibitedly pursue sex with as many women as humanly possible while caring little or nothing about the consequences of their actions. They believed that forsaking the principle of sexual discipline in women would release the floodgates, leading to free love and transform men into sexually addicted creatures who would violently yearn to fulfill their every sexual desire, uninhibitedly leading men to no longer see women as wives but as sexual beings to be conquered.

Chapter 13

Family Protection

This is another one of those cast-off relationship principles that society once put in place to protect women against romantic illusions and unworthy men. Unfortunately, the misinterpretation of family protection forced women into perceiving it as one more way of controlling and oppressing them. Although both parents enforced that principle, today's society views it as misogynistic; men presume women are the weaker sex, pitifully incapable of making rational decisions, and unable to protect themselves physically and emotionally. However, I believe family is the most extraordinary power of all. I wholeheartedly accept that, if a woman believes she doesn't need any romantic protection, then that's her absolute right and principle.

In the past, however, families thought it was their duty to protect their daughters' most prized and valuable possessions—their virtue from physical, sexual, and emotional abuse. I'm not arguing that abuse doesn't often happen in families, but the premise of the family was and still is a place of refuge.

Families understood their daughter's romantic and sexual lives had value and worth. They believed their daughter's mental, physical, and sexual virtue required protection from the ruthlessly cunning wolves at their daughters' gates, unworthy men who lacked integrity, conviction, or any moral standing.

Families knew that, if their daughters foolishly allowed guileful men beyond their walls, they would most likely kill, destroy, or cause significant damage beyond repair, leaving nothing but pain, mental depression, emotional heartbreak, anger, bitterness, and the stain of shame on their daughters' virtue, which would probably last a lifetime.

Once again, I'm not suggesting women can't protect their hearts—that would be imprudent and sexist of me. But romance can cloud one's judgment by allowing all the things that should be red flags to get overlooked repeatedly or dimmed by the bright lights that romantic physical and passionate gratification brings.

Romantic Love Often Blinds

People often put on blinders that refocus or narrow their vision, beliefs, or interpretations into what's known as tunnel vision: the ability to see only what's in front of them, whether true or false, in pursuit of their goals or destination. The flaw in tunnel vision is that it blocks access to other relevant information needed to make informed, fact-based decisions, which can lead to catastrophic conclusions.

A girl's family protection allowed men to self-evaluate and self-correct, to see whether they were worthy enough to present themselves and declare their intentions. It also meant they understood her family was her shield, her first and last line of defense, and saturated with the values they had taught her.

With confidence firmly established and ready for a life of marriage, men humbly accepted the process of being properly vetted to verify the truthfulness of their declarations and intentions. Family protection also meant all suitors had an awareness of fear, knowing that, if they violated the requested role as future husband and protector and allowed themselves to become abusive and dishonorable in any form, the same harsh brutality done to their daughter would be visited upon them by her family.

Today's new feminist consciousness states that a woman doesn't need family protection, and no one should ever tell a woman what to do, which is considered sexist. Regretfully, women have become blind to losing the critical protection family offers, as well as the healing of unconditional love.

There are no prerequisites concerning who your family should be, whether related by blood, adoption, or just friends that make up your tribe. We all need the protection of those who'll love us unconditionally enough to tell us the truth, whether we want to hear it or not, and still be there to help us pick up the broken fragments of our lives when we make mistakes.

Kissing Frogs

How many frogs have you kissed or had sex with that you thought were your prince? Don't you wish you had someone with whom romance or passion didn't impair their judgment, who would have helped you protect yourself against kissing unworthy, good-for-nothing, waste-of-time-in-bed sons of bitches? The mentality of arrogantly insisting you want to learn from your own bad experiences is stupid and overrated. You don't have to moronically stick your hand into the fire when you can see what happened to those who did.

Without family protection, you'll unwittingly place yourself in the line of fire to be mentally, emotionally, and physically abused. Being romantically unprotected makes you unconsciously naïve about the predators who see you as weak and vulnerable, instinctively granting them the right to hunt you as prey to fulfill their sexual desires, wants, and needs, without the fear of any accountability and repercussion because there's no one to protect you.

Hand in Marriage

The traditional practice of a man asking a girl's father for his daughter's hand in marriage wasn't sexist. Men understood there was a structure in place more significant than themselves and an authority that demanded their respect and honor. If they refused to follow the relationship's social norms or had no respect for the leadership in that girl's life, which was her father's and her family's values, they would have been found unworthy of pursuing her. And if he broke protocol, her family would believe he'd eventually visit that same disrespect on their daughter as his wife.

90

If a man has love, honor, and respect for you as a woman of worth, he would be enthusiastic about meeting your parents, family, and friends—and reluctantly happy to face the judgment of being vetted to see whether they would consider him worthy of dating, being in a relationship, or possibly marrying you.

The men you desire should have no reservations about allowing your family to verify whether they possess the potential qualities you need to become your future husband, spiritual inspiration, and protector—the kind of man worthy of taking your father's place as your first love.

Your family's vetting will make men think twice about coming into your life without good intentions and save you from a life of kissing unworthy frogs.

Chapter 14

An Equation of Love

Dating (no obligations): finding commonality + love =
A Relationship (a promise of fidelity) + building the relationship foundation = **Marriage** (genuine commitment)

There's nothing in this world that a mathematical equation or algorithm can't explain, like Isaac Newton's Law of Force: mass times acceleration (F = ma). Water is a compound formed by the chemical reaction of two hydrogen atoms and one oxygen atom (H2O). For instance, if you desired a slice of cheesecake, you'd expect some form of cheese in the cheesecake. If you want oatmeal cookies, you'd presume oatmeal is the main ingredient. Yet, for some strange reason, when we desire true, deep, everlasting love, we inadvertently forsake or imprudently leave out all the elements needed for the natural reactionary process to create love. And why? The path we willingly choose has allowed us to believe it's acceptable to put the cart before the horse.

We jump headfirst into sexual relationships and try to figure out who these people are while simultaneously demanding their love and loyalty.

This unacceptable indifference has left us in emotional bewilderment, wondering why our relationships keep failing or stagnating. Yet, somehow, we carelessly keep making the same mistake of not requiring a prerequisite promise of fidelity, leading to a commitment from our sexual partners. Yes, there should be no—I repeat, no—mitigating exceptions.

Dating is Not a Relationship

Before the 1900s, during the colonial era, there was no concept of dating; instead, a tradition of courtship prevailed. (Weigel, 1984).

When a man wanted to marry a woman, he declared his intentions to her family. A short, supervised romance ensued, followed by marriage.

There was no:

- "Well, I need five to seven years to get to know a person before I contemplate marriage."
- "We must live together first."
- "We have to see if we're sexually compatible."

Dating is not a relationship; too often, we muddy the waters between the two. Courtship/dating is part of the training process that adolescents or young adults use to develop their mental, emotional, spiritual, and sexual attraction toward potential mates who demonstrate the same moral principles and characteristics instilled within them by their families.

Yes, we all know physical attraction plays a significant role in desirability, but it shouldn't be the first — and only — quality we look for in a person. Physical attraction, if not properly managed, can impair one's ability to discern potential red flags and false truths as warning signs that we're developing poor decision-making habits when choosing a mate. Poor decision-making habits are why family protection, void of any romantic notions, was so crucial during the courting/dating process in the past.

The difference in dating as compared to a relationship is that there should never be any expectations, which include any sexual indulgences whatsoever. The ideology that, after a few dates, sex is imperative is a diabolical lie, and you should never feel obliged to conform to that false reality as a woman or man. You have the absolute, God-given right and freedom to date as many people as you want, without fear, guilt, or social harassment, which goes for both men and women alike. Engaging in sexual activities with someone you've just met and don't know is your choice and prerogative. However, and as cruel as this may seem, the people you choose to have sex with have no obligation to go out with you again or grant you any explanation whatsoever.

Your emotions, your need for answers, closure, or notions of right or wrong, have nothing to do with it; that's their unilateral privilege. I'm sorry if that shatters your fragile egotistical reality; that's just the cold, harsh truth of dating. As I've mentioned before, there should be no expectations or obligations in a dating relationship.

Dating facilitates the discovery of oneself by unearthing what you're attracted to, what you will or will not accept, and what you need in a future partner. It should provide the necessary skill set to guide you in your quest to find love, a relationship, and marriage.

You may initially find yourself attracted to only handsome, sexy men or beautiful girls, but after a few dates, you quickly realize that cute and dumb aren't that attractive.

You may then recognize that an intelligent conversation means more to you than a pretty face, and that strength of character, responsibility, and honor are the things that make a man or woman sexier and more desirable to you than a person's physique. The maturity of your dating skill set will guide your decisions regarding your choice of a potential mate who will enthusiastically help you lay the essential relationship foundations that your future marriage will require.

A Relationship is Exclusive Dating

- A relationship signifies that you've found someone worthy of your love, joy, and happiness.

- It's a pledge of fidelity with conditions.

- It's a declaration to forsake and not entertain other significant romantic curiosities, ensuring no physical, emotional, sexual, or financial abuse of each other.

- It has a clear vision for the future and the lucidity to establish a strong relationship foundation upon which you can build a future commitment together.

- It should come with an unmistakable comprehension that any breach of that promise of fidelity will determine the relationship's fate.

- And, most significantly, the security of exclusive dating should carry an expiration date.

Please understand that if your partner has no clear vision for your future and isn't investing in the relationship as an equal partner. You should, without hesitation, get out, even though you may have invested your time, resources, body, and heart in unwavering loyalty, hoping for the same in return.

- You have the right to leave your relationship for whatever reason you deem legitimate.

- You have no obligation in any way, shape, or form to give your partner an explanation, whether truthful or not, as to why you're leaving the relationship.

Yes, I know this sounds emotionally cruel and extremely harsh, but that's your unadulterated right. No one tells a woman or man in an abusive relationship to inform their abusive partner that they're leaving the abusive relationship to avoid hurting their abusive partner's feelings; what the hell?

"What about closure? I need emotional closure!"

They lied; they cheated. Move on, for heaven's sake.

The misinterpretation of relationships remains the reason for all the problems and difficulties society faces today. We're the ones who keep confusing a promise of fidelity based on conditions with commitment. We act like we legally own or control our partners' lives.

- "Where were you?"
- "Why didn't you call or text me back?"
- "Let me see your phone."
- "What are your new passwords?"
- "It takes twenty minutes to get home from work; why are you an hour late?"
- "I don't want you going anywhere without me."
- "I don't want you dressing like that."
- "I don't want you looking at or talking to other people."
- "I don't want you hanging out with your friends or family."

You and your partner are equally responsible for the construction of your relationship foundation through the following:

- Accepting each other for who they are, warts and all.

- Acknowledging each other's inner values and strengths so you can evolve and adjust to the changes you and your partner need to form a better union.

- Remaining diligent in not allowing the love you share to be disrupted by issues; issues are just issues to be worked out.

- Developing a friendship that will blossom into what your future commitment will require it to be.

- Recognizing that there are plenty of other ways to express your love for each other besides sex.

- Engaging in the constant practice of communication skills, conflict resolution, and the humility to say sorry and offer forgiveness, so your first action or response will be to listen and not get angry.

- Developing sympathy so you can identify distress in each other.

- Honoring your promise of fidelity so you can develop the ability to transition into your future commitment.

These are a few fundamental relationship-building blocks you must lay to have a solid foundation for a possible future marriage.

If you choose not to invest quality time and energy in developing these aspects of your relationship, your promise of fidelity and future marriage will ultimately fail.

Please stop falling for the lie that you need to know everything about someone before you commit to marriage. That's the godawful excuse men use to string women along by dangling the hope of a future marriage at the end of a relationship rainbow.

Marriage is True Commitment

Fidelity is the path that leads to commitment; marriage is the gift of commitment that opens the doors for you to give yourself entirely to your partner. A relationship, exclusive dating, is not that; that's why you keep feeling used and abused and, subsequently, forced into accepting the pain caused by seeing your parasitic relationship as acceptable behavior, where one person is constantly giving. The other invariably takes instead of building together equally.

Suppose you keep being your partner's ride-or-die chick, giving him loyalty without marriage, along with the sensual sexual pleasures of your body. In that case, you'll wake up one day and realize you were deceived and blinded by the fact that there was never any hope or plans for your future with him. All you'll have is a long-term relationship that never goes anywhere because you gave away your kingdom and your milk for free. If no one has told you this before, let me be the first to say: the price for your worth and value is marriage —the gift of commitment. You're the milk, a prize worthy of being someone's wife.

Most people today find it much easier to find love through a dating service. They have no problem accepting the concept of allowing online dating companies they've never met to find someone unique and compatible to date, to fall in love with, and, hopefully, become their lifelong partner.

However, it would be best if you realized that those dating services use the same concept or algorithm as arranged marriages, which modern societies turn their noses up at.

Parents, priests, judges, and government officials used to do the same thing, matching sons and daughters with individuals they believed were a good match. They thought the couples would eventually find purpose, respect, and love.

We all understand the history and complexities of marriage, its diverse cultural expressions, and the phases it has undergone since the dawn of humanity. We also know and acknowledge that people and organizations have used and abused this institution to create gender inequalities, re-sulting in the traumatic suffering of individuals.

Let me pause for a second and say to those who've suffered and presently feel trapped or forced to stay in their marriage due to their religion, children, or lack of financial freedom: I'm truly sorry! I hope you'll find the strength and courage to make the necessary changes.

Throughout the ages, societies have subjugated women (to a greater extent than men) to the institution of marriage for sex, servitude, procreation, and political and fi-nancial protection, refusing them the power of choice. West-ern Europe and North America's governing bodies in the seventeenth century eventually established that a woman's time, skill set, ability to reproduce, worth, and value were crucial to building the family. Therefore, wives should be equitably compensated by their husbands if they're divorced.

Those past disparities are why civil commitment to marriage is essential and is legally protected by governments today.

Our misguided romantic notions of what we think marriage should entail need to be reexamined. Our belief structure will determine what we believe on this issue if you're of the following:

- **Religious:** You believe love is the foundation that marriage is built on because God has ordained it, and God is love.

- **State/nonreligious:** You believe it's a human right to marry the person you love legally.

- **Conspiracy theorists:** You see marriage as a for-profit institution and a burden forced on the natural order of mating or coupling between humans.

Many within society don't believe in or have given up on the institution of marriage. They want all the benefits of marriage in their relationships or domestic unions, but not the legal responsibilities that come with it.

According to the Centers for Disease Control and Prevention (2022), the national marriage and divorce rate trends from the year 2000 until the end of 2020 are as follows:

- **Marriages:** 1,676,911; marriage rate: 5.1 per 1,000 total population

- **Divorces:** 630,505; divorce rate: 2.3 per 1,000 population

The basis for their disenchantment is the belief that most marriages today end in divorce, which, if taken at face value, has some merit. Those statistics, however, don't account for why those couples married in the first place or for the foundation of their relationships before marriage.

We see the reasons behind divorce, like financial illegality, sexual infidelity, lack of appreciation, and so on, yet we need to analyze the relationship foundation of those marriages. If we do, we will realize their foundations were weak or unstable, or lacked the capacity and strength to sustain and nourish their marriages.

Trust, fidelity, friendship, appreciation, forgiveness, kindness, and financial responsibility are qualities we should practice and manifest in every aspect of our lives, eventually becoming the building blocks of a successful marriage.

Suppose those qualities don't exist within us, then we might need to acknowledge that we may not be good relationship material. And if we aren't good relationship material, we'll be incapable of building a relationship foundation with someone who can establish and support a future marriage.

The perfect romantic picture is one where a boy meets a girl, the girl meets the boy, they fall madly in love, and dating ensues, blossoming into a relationship that leads to marriage, children, and lasting happiness. However, this painful truth remains—if we're ill-prepared or have no desire to build a relationship foundation with someone but still want the emotional, physical, and financial benefits of a relationship or marriage, then we're not only lying and deceiving ourselves for our selfish gratification but also willfully lying and deceiving the people we claim to love.

The Guardians of Our Hearts

The relationship foundation is the safeguard that walls in and houses the strong tower that holds the vault that surrounds and protects the love that couples share for each other within their marriage. Hence, when life issues emerge and present themselves, as they naturally do, they would have learned through the laying of their foundation that issues are just issues to be worked out and have nothing to do with the love they share. I hope you grasp this vital relationship and marriage concept.

Suppose we become blinded by our selfish emotional desires and dangerously incapable of distinguishing our relationship conflicts from our partner's love as separate entities. In that case, we will unwittingly open the doors, allowing hate and animosity to take root in our marriages, thus destroying the foundation that leads to the love we share with our partners. Unresolved relationship conflicts are the primary reason many couples seek therapy. That's why old people say, "Never go to bed upset or angry with your partner."

Yet hope always remains, and, yes, rebuilding your marriage will seem like the most challenging thing you'll ever have to do, because, at present, you may not feel or share the love you once had—although that emotion might be your current conviction, not your future reality.

You owe it to yourself to fight for the life you've built by diligently working out your issues through honest communication, patience, kindness, standing your ground, and holding fast to the love you both believed in and once shared. And, yes, you can relearn how to separate your relationship issues and rebuild the foundation of your marriage. You can be each other's safe place, where vulnerability is permitted, granting you the freedom to express your inner thoughts and feelings without judgment and trust that you can always find comfort in each other's arms.

Legal Protection

Your status as a wife, which has been legally established and protected by law, gives you the right to pursue legal action against your husband's infidelities or any other woman who tries to alienate your husband's affection from you. There are no such legal benefits or protections for you to be someone's lover, girlfriend, or side chick. The gay community recognized that flaw in just being someone's relationship partner in the 1960s.

In the landmark case, *Obergefell v. Hodges*, the US Supreme Court ruled, "All State bans on same-sex marriage were unconstitutional, making gay marriage legal throughout America" (*Petitioners v. Richard Hodges, Director, Ohio Department of Health et al.*, 2015).

And why was that decision so important? Gay couples being hated and isolated from their families found themselves in situations where they had no legal or medical rights to intervene or represent their partners in life-or-death medical decisions, or weren't even allowed to visit them in the hospital. Only their partner's legal kin, who may or may not have loved or cared about them, had lawful authority. And, if they died, their family members were the only ones entitled to claim any financial wealth or benefits they left behind. On April 15, 2010, President Barack Obama released a Presidential Memorandum - Hospital Visitation, Respecting the Rights of Hospital Patients to Receive Visitors and

Designate Surrogate Decision Makers for Medical Emergencies:

- "By this memorandum, I request that you take the following steps. Initiate appropriate rulemaking under your authority and other relevant law provisions to ensure that hospitals participating in Medicare or Medicaid respect the rights of patients to designate visitors. It should be clear that selected visitors, including individuals set by legally valid advance directives, should enjoy visitation privileges that are no more restrictive than those that immediate family members want. You should also provide that participating hospitals may not deny visitation privileges based on race, color, national origin, religion, sex, sexual orientation, gender identity, or disability" (National Archives and Records Administration, 2010).

President Barack Obama began his Presidential Memorandum by stating:

- "Yet every day, across America, patients are denied the kindness and caring of loved ones at their sides— whether in a sudden medical emergency or a prolonged hospital stay. Often, a widow or widower with no children is denied the support and comfort of a good friend. Members of religious orders may not be able to choose someone other than an immediate family member to visit them and make medical decisions on their behalf. Also uniquely affected are gay and lesbian Americans, who are often barred from the bedsides of the partners with whom they may have spent decades of their lives—unable to be there for the person they love and unable to act as a legal surrogate if their partner is incapacitated" (National Archives and Records Administration, 2010).

Marriage is more than just companionship, sex, and a warm body at night. It's about respect, being chosen, legal protection, and the right to raise children within a loving, safe, harmonious environment filled with happiness, stability, and equal opportunity to build financial wealth. Wait a minute! What have I been thinking? In our discussion about marriage, I should have asked whether you want to get married; I honestly couldn't tell.

- You've allowed men to use your body for their erotic pleasures as a one-night stand, friends with benefits, or as placement holders in stupid-ass, dead-end relationships for five, ten, or fifteen years, without marriage.

- You've willingly given access to your womb to stupid, unworthy men who don't have a pot to piss in or a plate to stand on, to impregnate you, to plant their seeds, without marriage.

- You've allowed undeserving men who habitually lie and cheat and have no moral standards of honor and fidelity to disrespect you continually. Yet you consistently offer forgiveness and absolute loyalty, without the benefit of marriage.

- You've supported your lovers mentally and emotionally; you've become their rock, their strong tower, their place of comfort, their ride-or-die chick, without marriage.

- You become enraged and viciously jealous to the point where you physically attack other women when they seemingly become sexually attracted to your lover, without marriage.

- You criticize men for living at home with their parents, the mommy's boys; you deliberately choose men who live on their own, so you can selfishly weasel your way into shacking up, to nest, to play house, without marriage.

Your gifts, the sweet milk reserved for marriage only, have been graciously and freely given away to ineligible men for nothing in return.

Let me reemphasize what I've stated: there are no obligations in dating; a relationship is exclusive dating with a promise of fidelity, subject to conditions; and marriage is the only form of genuine relationship commitment.

What was that word I asked you to remember?

Oh yeah, choice!

Chapter 15

The Paradox of Fear, Sex, and Love

M any false relationship doctrines have permeated our collective consciousness; yet one concept has maneuvered freely as an accepted truth: the merger of love and fear. The truth is, these two possessive forces cannot coexist within the emotional constructs of our hearts and minds. Yet these two natural entities have been and can be falsely misinterpreted or promoted as the same passion within us. Therefore, our actions will be rooted in love or serving our fears, and they can become the stimulus that influences our mental and emotional relationship choices, which can carry blessings or consequences.

Jealousy is Fear

Anxiety, panic, and worry are all natural expressions of fear, but, within a relationship, fear is jealousy incarnate, masquerading as love.

We've been brainwashed and led to believe our jealousy is a profound expression of our love toward our partners or that our lover's jealousy signifies how much they truly love us.

This false, misguided reality is a lie because love and fear cannot coexist within us.

"And no one can serve two masters" (*New International Version*, Matthew 6:24).

There's a story in the Bible about a man named Job, which centers on love and fear. He allowed his relationship with God, which was supposed to be rooted in love, to become toxic, thanks to an obsessive fear.

So, God permitted everything Job feared losing—his children and wealth—to become his reality.

And once his terror became his actuality, the false God of fear that had possessed him ceased to exist—revealing that his relationship with the intelligent design, the God of his forefathers, should only be based on unconditional love.

Our phobia of losing what we so desperately desire drives us to dominate our partners viciously and unsympathetically, by any means necessary, and regardless of who ultimately gets hurt. We unconsciously subject our partners to our harmful insecurities by creating false figments in our imagination, which can, regrettably, lead to abusive relationships. Unfortunately, confusing jealousy with love and allowing our mental faculties to entertain a suspicious, possessive nature can lead to a permissible state of mind where our unbridled freedom enables us to value the emotional highs of sexual pleasures, financial benefits, and the superficial attributes of our relationships above ourselves and our partners.

Our narcissistic belief, our paranoia of loss, can also become the unseen force propelling us to manipulate our partners into believing they should be grateful that we've allowed them to be in a relationship with us while simultaneously promoting the belief that the emotional emptiness we've been experiencing is just our natural yearning to love or to be loved and that all our intentional actions or inactions are justifiable. All these forces — the jealousy, the fear of loss, and the unbearable, carnivorous pain of loneliness — are the stimuli behind our undisciplined desires, which we deliberately use to seek out the kind of parasitic relationships we want. This form of self-manipulation begins the moment our inner fears meet potential victims by disguising our wants as the qualities we seek in a person, which are not qualities at all. We then become so enthralled by having our shallow desires met that we don't even see the toxic jealousy, the paranoia of fear, the domination, or maltreatment happening within our relationship. All we choose to see or interpret is love.

Our misguided romantic delusions based on fear can cause our personality to transform and alter our emotional perceptions, which forces us to become dogmatically fixated on issues like the following:

- **Sexual betrayal:** Becoming furious at the thought that our lover may be admiring other people or sexually active with someone else.

- **Our partner's appearance:** The way our partner dresses may now be too sexy or attract too much attention.

- **Associations:** Who our partners' friends are.

- **Location:** Where they go and what time they return home.

- **Social media:** Who they communicate with, what they post, and who they like or don't like.

115

We may even find ourselves constantly accusing our lovers of infidelity, based on feelings, yet we feel little or no remorse concerning our sexual betrayals, adultery, and affairs.

Let's take a closer look at some of the tangible and intangible things we may be afraid of losing in our relationships—the things our jealousy and our fear of loss employ to force us to become submissive, passive-aggressive, or domineering:

- **Title or identity:** Losing the prestige of your partner's career or position if they're a doctor, politician, lawyer, pastor, professional sports star, music recording artist, movie star, or swimsuit model

- **Intimacy:** The painful thought of being alone and living with the constant anxiety, your partner might realize you're nothing without them or that they're more robust and better off without you

- **Financial vulnerability:** Either becoming controlling or submissive, so you don't lose the economic benefits and lifestyle attained from the relationship

- **Vision manipulation:** Suppressing your partner's ability to perceive jealousy as controlling but as deep, passionate love

Ironically, the things we're terrified of have nothing to do with love, and that's why those who act out of fear are either quick to offer unconditional forgiveness for their partner's transgressions or demand the same for themselves.

They unconsciously calculate the value of their indiscretions or offenses against what they stand to lose. So, they either become abusive, passive, or submissive to justify their infractions or their partner's violations by blaming themselves or falsely accusing the ones they claim to love. Their controlling nature will eventually deplete their partner's mental and emotional resources, resulting in what will ultimately happen: they'll leave or find love, comfort, and pleasure in someone else's arms.

Forcing or tempting your partner to act out of character never bodes well for your relationship.

Your impaired vision, elicited by your fear, leads to the skewing of rational thinking to the point where you now wholeheartedly believe your actions were not responsible for the collapse of your relationship.

Your righteous indignations leave you confident that your relationship problems were all caused by your partner's inability to accept your love. The delusional reality of your partner's betrayal now leads you to seek vengeance through the following:

- **Child abandonment:** Financially withholding child support, not granting parental visitation, or lawfully trying to take the children away

- **Defamation:** Posting falsehoods or illicit pictures on social media

- **Felonious falsification:** Trying to have them arrested for physical abuse, rape, or child endangerment

- **Harassment:** Tracking your ex's every move and turning up unannounced

- **Psychological manipulation:** Creating doubt in your partner's mind by saying the child isn't theirs, whether truthful or not, to hurt them

- **Vandalism:** The destruction of property or the pillaging of their material belongings and finances

- **Sexual retaliation:** Trying to hurt them by sleeping with one of their family members or close friends

- **Dissolution of employment:** Having them fired

So, What is Love?

True love compels.

It requires acknowledging the person we are with as our equal and treating them with the same honor, respect, and dignity we believe we deserve.

It also unleashes a fierce, natural instinctive protectionism in men, causing some women to feel unequal or incapable, but that is far from the truth.

That protective nature allows men to see women as precious, valued creatures, worthy of kindness and compassion. This vision of worthiness gave birth to what we interpret as chivalry—the willingness of men to work their fingers to the bone to provide.

That same love also unleashes that exact protective nature in women toward their partners and children. If someone hits your child, I know you'll be ready to burn the entire world down to the ground with everyone in it to protect them.

We must also realize this protective nature can quickly become corrupted by fear masquerading as love, which is no longer about protecting those we love but possessively controlling them.

However, if we take the time to listen, we'll realize the following:

- **Love is kind:** It considers the feelings and opinions of those we're involved with, based on their reality.

- **Love is patient:** It allows us to develop our ability and capacity to show compassion.

- **Love forgives:** It allows us to forgive those who trespass against us. However, it doesn't demand we forgive those unworthy of forgiveness; that's our right and will. It requests that we not return for a second or third helping of the abuse and suffering.

- **Love offers self-forgiveness:** It unburdens us from the guilt and shame inflicted by past transgressions and poor choices.

- **Love heals:** It compassionately compels us to take the time to heal and become armed and shielded with the strength and courage to avoid repeating the same mistakes.

- **Love protects:** It flashes neon signs of danger, alerting us to be cautious.

- **Love sets standards:** It allows us to establish disciplined distinctions based on morality and family values. It enables us only to entertain those who display a similar moral compass worthy of our love, joy, and happiness.

-

A Wuk-up is Just a Wuk-up

(Barbadian Dialect)

In other words, sex is just sex between two or more consenting adults. But, unfortunately, people often complicate the quenching of one's physical desires with love.

Notwithstanding, if sex is love or an expression of love, then every one-night stand, friends with benefits, extramarital affair, male or female prostitute, call girl, or gigolo would be in love with every one of their sexual partners.

Only two things influence our sexual encounters:

The Packaging

- A person's physical attributes, superficial beauty
- Their values and morals

The Motives

- Emotional connections or material gains
- Sexual lust or procreation

We often tend to sexually desire those we consider beautiful, hot, or sexy, those whose physical attributes turn us on by making our emotional and sexual blood boil with infatuation. However, if we stop for a moment and look back at our past sexual encounters, we realize some of our most incredible sexual experiences weren't just with those who were hot and sexy but also with those who were sweet, kind, or less attractive. Often, they're the ones with whom we've had the most romantic and profound, unexpected sexual experiences.

The reality is, we're the ones who ascribe relevance to our sexual encounters, regardless of which tool we use to determine our sexual interactions, the packaging, or the motives.

If we took away the packaging or the reasons, we would still conclude that sex, even mind-blowing, leg-shaking, slap-your-mama sex, is just sex, and as I have stated before, every prostitute, one-night stand, friend with benefits, side chick, or side guy would all be in love after their sexual encounters, but it has nothing to do with love; it's just sex.

Sex is Not a Manifestation of Love

Look, I'm not trying to trivialize our natural proclivities toward sex. I'm trying to get you to acknowledge that we must destroy the false relationship doctrine that has led us to believe sex is a physical manifestation of love.

Our learned attributes, like love, fidelity, commitment, honor, respect, kindness, sympathy, and forgiveness, have no connections to sex. Therefore, sex is not an attribute or a physical expression of these qualities. It never was, and we should never have made that mistake. Yet we must learn to connect sex to these essential qualities within our relationships.

"Wait, what? You just said sex has no connection to love, fidelity, or commitment?"

Yes, that's true; let me explain this paradox. As I've noted, if sex is love or an expression of love, then every sexual encounter with a hooker would be an expression of love, but they aren't. Sex is just sex.

So, with that supposition clearly in mind, let me argue that sex should be a benefit of fidelity and commitment within a relationship.

We've discussed how sex was one of those traditional relationship principles reserved for marriage, and it was for the discipline of men so that they could honor the principle of commitment. I know this sounds counterintuitive to what we've been indulging in as modern-day relationship principles, but sex was supposed to be the following:

- A benefit of a proven promise of fidelity
- A gift of verified love

- A blessing and one of the many pleasures of commitment

So why should sex be a benefit? Sex can emotionally blind us from seeing or acknowledging that our lover's intense sexual desire for us may have nothing to do with love, fidelity, commitment, beauty, or desirability. It just might be their illicit sexual disregard for morality wrapped up in misguided emotions we keep accepting as true love.

We often fail to comprehend that sex is not a right or a given. It is, and should always be, an earned benefit of the attributes given or received. This is how sex becomes intertwined with love, fidelity, and commitment in our relationships. This goes directly to the heart of what I'm trying to get you to discern.

Suppose one of the many benefits of proven love, fidelity, and commitment within your relationship is sex. In that case, your passion and dedication toward each other should not change or fade away based on the frequency or scarcity of your sexual activity.

Let me reemphasize this certitude. The frequency or lack of sexual activity within your relationships should not affect your love, fidelity, and commitment because they're independent.

Many couples often build their relationships and marriages on the sands of lust and sex. And when those foundations are washed away by the pounding tides of life's storms, and their sexual lives become ordinary, they find themselves having nothing in common and lacking the ability to express what they don't have, which is love.

Regrettably, many relationships fall apart because there's nothing else to sustain the relationship or marriage.

This conscious realization brings many couples to the point where they must accept they had tragically confused great sex as deep, passionate love.

The failure to teach individuals to associate sex with fidelity and commitment is one of society's relationship sins, and, without those connections, true love cannot exist.

To obtain the passion and dedication you desire, you must demand from men who want to taste the sweet nectar of your bodies that they must prove they're worthy of you through acts of verified love, confirmed fidelity, and demonstrated commitment. To achieve these objectives, you will need to do the following:

- Stop being sexually indiscriminate: "I know, off with my head." I'm not asking you to stop having sex; you're a grown-ass woman, and no one should ever tell a grown-ass woman what to do with her body. I'm just suggesting you stop being a willing participant in the inexcusable sexual exploits of men.

- Stop giving in to the desperation of wanting a man, any man.

- Allow men to recognize and comprehend that you're a woman of standards, possessing the quality worthy of being someone's wife.

We're the ones who foolishly choose not to arm ourselves with the knowledge to understand the difference between lust and love.

Sex is only one of the many benefits of the totality of our relationships. This lack of discernment is why many of our relationships and marriages are in emotional turmoil today.

Therefore, this remains our charge: we must change our mindset by developing the necessary relationship skills, requiring love and fidelity as prerequisites for courtship, relationships, and marriage, with no exceptions.

Chapter 16

The Scent of Despair

We tend to desire those whose physical attributes turn us on sexually. This tantalizing lust compels our primal nature to seek short- or long-term companionship or to hunt sexually.

We've seen *the National Geographic* nature shows where predators hunt their prey. Unfortunately, we overlook the innate behavior of predators who are opportunists who prefer to pursue those they consider weak, old, sick, or injured. And on rare, desperate occasions or when the chance presents itself, they'll hunt the strong. Predators also understand and acknowledge the ability of prey animals to recognize that there's strength in numbers, so their tactical strategy is to ambush their prey through isolation.

Prey animals constantly rely on their innate skill set to recognize the presence of predators in their immediate surroundings, using their senses of sight, smell, and hearing, along with speed, to keep them safe.

All men have the same innate potential to become romantic predators if they can't control their inner demons. The lack of self-discipline in men leads them to become enthralled by the thrill of the hunt. Their awakened lustful desire is to bathe in the sexual pleasures of weak, consenting prey while marinating in the memories of past conquests.

The behaviors of romantic predatory men often appear as flattery toward women. Unfortunately, this deception inflates women's egos into misperceiving predatory attention as their sexual desirability. Conceitedly, women design the value of their lives based on that false, accepted self-confidence that they're beautiful, hot, and sexy, yet completely unaware that all the intense interest from men only means one thing: they're sexual prey. The desire to be wanted impulsively guides women's physical and sexual attractions toward opportunistic, romantic, predatory men who have the ability and resources to fulfill the materialistic lifestyle they believe they deserve. Here's another question of contemplation: why haven't the men you've allowed in your bed stuck around after they enjoyed the sexual fruits of your body?

Once again, I'm not imploring you to stop having sex; by all means, spread your legs and give away sweet erotic pleasure to all, near and far, if you want to. But you must know you're allowing men without honorable intentions to hunt, capture, and unreservedly conquer you. And why? You have unconsciously decided that your only source of self-confidence and strength comes from your proudly displayed physical appearance, and the ill-advised gesticulating of your physical beauty materializes like a floodlight to predatory men, who then see you as arrogant and weak.

The hidden emotional anxiety complex that makes you constantly feel like you're being sexually used and abused by men doesn't have to be your continued reality. It would help if you recognized that it's your responsibility to develop the physical, mental, and emotional survival skills of prey animals. Your survival skill set will allow you to protect yourself against romantic predatory men, knowing when to stand your ground and fight or when to run away.

Men know what you'll be to them from the moment they look at you. Regrettably, suppose you continue to operate out of desperation, casually having sex without realistic standards and not vigorously demanding that men correct their learned bad behavior of wanting sex without proven love, fidelity, and commitment.

In that case, they'll continue to cheat and sexually prey upon you.

The Sisterhood of Accountability

Women must also hold their female contemporaries accountable for allowing their bodies to become the sexual playground of romantic, predatory men. The continued irresponsible behavior of some women has come at a high cost to the moral fiber of fidelity in relationships. Promiscuity is why some women struggle to find good men within the sea of so much unfaithfulness. Men who may have once honored their values by being committed to their relationships and children now find themselves in a sexual playground with countless morally bankrupt, willing participants. Why should any man want to or willingly choose to be committed to any woman when he can effortlessly get all the milk and sweet sexual nectar from a profusion of women for free?

I still don't understand why you're allowing men you don't know, men you haven't vetted, and men who have no sign of proven values and morals into your heart, your bed, and your children's lives. What also baffles and seems almost comical is that you repeatedly allow yourself to become impregnated by those same weak-ass men.

You then turn and become infuriated that those same romantic predatory men consistently deny being the fathers of your children and angrily refuse to step up to the plate and take care of their responsibilities. These men never had plates, to begin with; seriously, what the hell?

You're the ones who keep letting the dogs, the deadbeats, and the no-good, non-committed romantic predators into your lives. You keep succumbing foolishly to the emptiness of being alone and wanting companionship, regardless of the cost. Your undisciplined thirst for sexual gratification, the fear of missing out, the thrill of reckless behavior, and the consequence of one wrong decision after the next have left you mentally and emotionally damaged, which is the actual cost of desperation. Remember, your body, your choice!

The Blame Game

The emotional scars and the bitterness created by the kissing of so many ignoble frogs have blinded you to the fact that your continued amoral dating relationship habits and choices in men will ultimately lead you to the path of the blame game, and who keeps getting the blame for all the hurt and pain caused by your choices? —Men.

Currently, there are many forms of quality birth control; why are you and your daughters still having unplanned, unwanted, and out-of-wedlock pregnancies, which force you to make the agonizing choice of having an abortion, and, in the aftermath, quietly live with the excruciating pain and inner turmoil to define what that decision means?

To this, I would like to say, "I'm sorry." If no one has ever told you—but I think you already know—don't put yourself in a position where you can get pregnant from a sexual encounter with a man, especially careless men who, amid your sexual romantic bliss, utter the words, "I want you to have my baby."

Reproductive Responsibility

I don't know when it happened or who in society led some women to believe it's only their bodies and their choices regarding abortions, and not their responsibility to protect their reproductive capabilities by using scientifically proven birth control. Once again: sex doesn't have to lead to pregnancy; you control your reproductive destiny.

Let me state some facts you already know:

- You and your daughters have the absolute right to use any form of birth control you want.

- You have the undiluted right to force your sexual partners to wear condoms; that isn't their choice; it's yours. Let me repeat that last statement. Men don't have the right to choose not to wear condoms; that singular responsibility is yours and yours alone.

And for the love of everything holy, please stop using and regurgitating those dumb, imprudent excuses you and your friends have used to justify your dereliction of sexual responsibility and self-discipline:

- "My lover and I don't particularly appreciate how condoms make us feel."

- "He said he wanted to experience and taste my true sexual essence."

- "If my man wears condoms when we have sex, it makes me think I might not be his one and only. I'm not a side chick."

- "Our passion took us; we couldn't control ourselves."

- "He told me he loved me."

- "We were drunk."

Please stop listening to your friends' irresponsible dating advice, especially from those who aren't married or struggle to maintain a relationship. Understand that those reckless Instagram posts that declare what your romantic lives should be are fictitious. If you continue to let these things affect your emotional stability, they'll make you desperate. Unfortunately, that scent of desperation permeating from your despair will signal to all romantic predatory men that you're weak, emotionally wounded, and ready to be hunted. Your desire to be wanted, if not controlled, will undoubtedly engulf your intuition from discerning that the men you choose as sexual partners are just using you as an object of masturbation. There's nothing wrong with wanting a relationship or sex. Unfortunately, desires fueled by desperation lead to the troubles relationships face today: lying, unfaithfulness, and the fear of commitment. You're the ones who control and sustain the sexual playground of men. You have allowed men to run sexually wild by your willingness to let sex be just sex without setting any standards or moral guidelines. Here's a sexually disciplined principle that I think both men and women should consider. No use of birth control or sexual protection means no sexual activity. Yes, it may seem a bit unrealistic, but it's still worth considering. Then again, I may be wrong; you may be benefiting from this relationship chaos.

Chapter 17

The Rights of Women

"Women's rights are human rights."
(United Nations Human Rights Office, 2014).

I believe it's a woman's right to choose what happens to her body, along with all the other medical decisions she makes regarding her mental and emotional well-being. No man, group, religion, or state should have the right to tell a woman what to do with her own body; we've been down that awful abortion road before, where financially challenged women had to venture into the dark recesses of society. In comparison, their affluent counterparts could afford the luxuries of physicians and the quieting of public shame. Many communities have conveniently ignored that there was a class of women sold as enslaved people around the world, with no rights to their bodies, and, at the same time, the wives of their enslavers had a seat at the table of power. Enslaved women worked the fields, did the domestic work, and were bred like cattle while breastfeeding their enslavers' babies and fulfilling every illicit sexual desire their masters and wives wanted; this happened no matter what age the girls were, including young boys and men.

There was no recourse or psychological treatments for those who suffered sexual abuse, nor any therapy for the emotional pain and suffering caused to parents by having their children ripped from their tired arms and sold into servitude and never seen again (Library of Congress, n.d.).

Dr. J. Marion Sims ("Marion J. Sims," 2022) was an Alabama surgeon known as the father of gynecology, and he conducted experimental operations on enslaved Black women between 1845 and 1849. Many authors condemn Sim's medical ethics because he manipulated the institution of slavery to perform unethical human experiments without anesthesia on powerless, enslaved Black women in a small hospital in Montgomery, Alabama, trying to cure vesicovaginal fistulas. Sims operated thirty times on a young, enslaved woman named "Anarcha" with an allegedly challenging combination of vesicovaginal and rectovaginal fistula, hoping to close the holes in her bladder and rectum.

Sadly, and unfortunately, to this very day, the descendants of those enslaved still struggle with an inherited, indoctrinated generational psychological disability of identity loss—an identity destroyed by those who sought to elevate their cultural and financial superiority around the world.

The brainwashing of women of color forced them to believe the following:

- Their dark skin wasn't beautiful.

- Their hair was too kinky and would never be acceptable.

- Their large lips, big breasts, wide hips, and voluptuous butts were unattractive features.

- Their lives had no value; they were deemed only worthy of domestic duties.

- They should sit in the back of the bus and use Colored-only restrooms, restaurants, and separate entrances because their station in life was less than that of others in society.

And when they got the opportunity to work within specific industries, they were forced to change their appearance to look like their White peers.

These are some of the same reasons women of color, to this present day, still adorn themselves with fake accouterments, theoretically trying to fit into someone else's artificial standards of beauty.

I'm terrified this sustained psychological damage may never heal because the infected wounds caused by the diabolical, prejudicial implementations that were deliberately left untreated and institutionalized have now morphed into what we have today: an inherited curse of identity loss.

Women of all nationalities have been fighting and dying for their civil rights for centuries, challenging outdated judicial systems and achieving many of their stated objectives. However, some organizations still fight to roll back the progress that has been made.

Chapter 18

Value Structure and
Self-Discipline

In the past, women saw themselves as being virtuous when they embodied the following:

- **Confidence:** Taking pride in their attire and how others perceive them

- **Disciplined:** Having self-control in all aspects of their lives

- **Ethics:** Possessing morals, values, and principles

- **Intelligent:** Being informed

- **Self-worth:** Seeing their inner qualities as their true beauty and desirability, worthy of marriage

Your self-awareness as a woman of substance will give you the confidence to focus your skill set on crafting an accurate depiction of who you are. This established, directed perception will command respect and dignity and force romantic predatory men, the dogs of sexual war, to run away.

There's a big difference between how you treat a Mercedes-Benz and a scooter, a pair of Christian Louboutin shoes, and a pair of Payless slippers. In other words, the same way you place a high value on brand-name apparel applies; you and your daughters must develop the aptitude to proudly acknowledge your realistic self-worth to minimize the possibility of allowing unworthy men into your hearts.

Regrettably, some women operate in a state of ambiguity, lacking a moral compass or a clear value structure to guide their path. This failure of guidance ushers in a mentality of anything goes when pursuing love, joy, and happiness in men, who often proclaim what women want to hear.

Failed sexual relationships become crushing bags of heartaches and regrets, which visually impair some women's ability to see that they've been dragging emotionally unhealthy bags as ship anchors into every new relationship.

You're responsible for developing a structure of self-discipline to control your emotions and desires, which will help you alleviate some of the deplorable relationship pitfalls you'll face in this life. The disregard for the principle of feminine sexual self-discipline opened the doors for men to abandon self-regulations that were always influenced by and connected to the established standards of women.

"But why should the sexual discipline of men be our responsibility as women?"

I admit this is a heavy burden to place on modern women, as society holds everyone responsible for their actions. However, the reality is that this forsaken responsibility has always been, still is, and will always be the burden of women to bear, regardless of how you may feel.

As I stated at the beginning of our discussion, you control the sexual playground of men, and they need your consent and permission to play.

Suppose you genuinely desire the kind of relationships you believe you deserve. In that case, women, collectively, must once again take up the mantle of sexual responsibility and self-discipline so men can no longer find free sex but are forced to accept sex as one of the many benefits of fidelity and commitment.

Chapter 19

The Veiled Road of Communication

You think men don't communicate, but you're mistaken. The problem is you conveniently choose not to listen.

- If a man tells you he doesn't want kids, he's communicating he doesn't want kids.

- When a man tells you he doesn't want a relationship, he's expressing he's not that into you and, therefore, will not invest any emotions, time, or energy into you, except maybe sexually.

- When you discover other women's phone numbers, photos, or romantic messages on his social media, he's communicating that he's trying to hook up with other women.

- If you catch him cheating, he's communicating that he doesn't want you; he wants to be with other women.

- If he spends most of his time with friends rather than with you, he's communicating that he finds happiness and joy in being with other people, rather than with you.

- If he's constantly lying about everything, he's communicating that he doesn't respect or care about you and your feelings.

- If he doesn't allow you to meet his friends, family, or kids, he's communicating that you aren't significant to him.

- If he doesn't give you a vision for your future together, he's communicating that you'll never have a leading role in any of his plans.

- If you find yourself stuck in a long-term relationship, and he hasn't asked you to marry him, he's communicating that you're just a placeholder, a warm bed at night, a provider of regular sex he can use until he can find someone better.

But what do you hear and interpret?

"He wants me to change him," or "Once he gets to know me, that will all change."

Should I go on? Communication means you must listen. It doesn't give you the right to hear what you want to hear or to interpret what you want to believe, because it fits your romantic notions and delusional narratives. That's why emotionally hurt women often seek out those complicit in regurgitating the same lousy relationship information they want to hear for comfort and solidarity.

- "Girl, you know men are stupid; he's acting out; he can't handle your love."

- "It's those other bitches going after your man; he knows where home is."

- "You need to make him suffer like you're suffering; if he can sleep around with other people, you can sleep around too."

Egos

Women have the same or even bigger egos than men. And your pride, like men, sometimes gets in the way of your happiness.

You'll fight to the death to keep a lousy relationship alive, even though all the signs alert you, without prejudice, that the relationship is already dead, all because you don't want to lose, especially to other women. "But I love him."

Joy, Happiness, and Love

These attributes exist within us, and it's our responsibility to cultivate and experience their full richness so we can become our genuine, complete selves, understanding that we don't need to seek those qualities in others to make us whole. Instead, we should share our inner peace with those who genuinely deserve it.

The lack of these undeveloped qualities often impairs our ability to recognize good men and women, leading us to make questionable relationship choices in an attempt to quench our desires. This emptiness is why some women, unwillingly, accept the false relationship doctrine that guys who work all the time and don't go clubbing every weekend—or who refuse to spend most of their money on cars, clothes, jewelry, and women—are uninteresting. These are the types of men women don't want, the ones they friend-zone, string along, and call on—when the ones they genuinely desire are incompetent.

145

Your sole desire or sexual attraction, which you have allowed yourself to develop, is only for the bad boys. And why?

Because everything about them seems so exciting, including the temporary fulfillment of your undeveloped feelings of joy, happiness, and love.

- You get to be sexually free, emotionally wild, and reckless.

- He aggressively grabs you and tells you what he wants.

- Your lover treats you like a sex toy or a prostitute.

- Your arguments lead to intense, passionate make-up sex.

- You enjoy the drama of fighting off other women who want him.

- You're excited by nightclubs, drinking, and drugs.

- He makes you feel wanted and needed because he relies on you for things like money, your car, or a place to stay.

This temporary gratification seems extremely exciting until your ass gets pregnant, and then, miraculously, the true enlightenment of responsibility kicks in. Your bad boy isn't attractive anymore since he called you a slut and a bitch and denied he's the one who got you pregnant.

Now, lo and behold, you realize you need a man who is stable and financially responsible. And, oh, who could that possibly be? "Please, let me answer that for you." It's Mr. Cheap, Mr. Boring, and Mr. Financially Responsible, the men you've constantly put in the friend zone who've been standing on their plates. The ones that some women will try to deceive into believing they're the fathers of their children.

Here are some of the questions you should be asking yourselves:

- Why don't ordinary working men, who don't care about peacocking but have discernment for their future, appeal to you?

- Why is the financial accountability of a man not an attractive quality in men for you?

- Why does it turn you off when a man demands you live within your financial means and doesn't believe in helping you pay your bills because you're supposed to be an adult? How is that not an attractive quality for you?

- Why does it turn you off when a man lives with his parents and pays rent, which keeps financial wealth

147

within his family? Why is that not an attractive quality to you?

Your indifference toward having a value structure and the ability to be guided by a moral compass has impaired your ability to attract good men that women in the past would have gladly chosen for themselves or their daughters. Society has conditioned some women to focus on the value men create rather than their inner qualities. Men's jobs, professions, financial wealth, and worldly possessions are the instruments now used to define and determine what a good man should be.

Chapter 20

The Puppet Master

One thing that constantly baffles me is that some women don't want to accept men for who they are. The impression society generally receives is that women persistently look for men with specific characteristics to change, manipulate, or makeover into the men of their dreams—the ones they can persuade to love how they want to be loved and be enthusiastic about granting them the romantic lifestyle they deserve. The idea or concept that a woman's prerogative or duty is to change or fix a man has become so baked into society's psyche that women still don't seem to realize it's never worked and never will. Yet they expect different results. This horrific scheme of manipulation has been perpetuated and regurgitated, along with all the other false philosophies, and has been about one thing and one thing only—control.

In your quest for what you believe is true love, have you ever tried to control every aspect of your relationships and your partner's life, hoping he would grant you the ultimate prize you so greatly desire—his love wrapped up in loyalty and commitment?

Your sanctioned desire to control every aspect of your relationship is the same egotistical behavior found in romantic predatory men, which forces you to practice the following deceitful concepts:

- **Isolation:** Separating your partner from his family and friends and attempting to eradicate all other women, including his mother, from his life

- **The redirection of thought processes and goals:** Manipulating him into believing you're the center of his universe

- **The monopolization of his time:** Persuading him to spend all his free time with you, constantly communicating and monitoring who he calls,, and obsessively checking his social media activity

- **Financial sway:** Becoming a significant part of his financial obligations

- **Modified behavior:** Using sexual pleasure as a reward for following your romantic and financial commands

- **Image adjustment:** Changing how he dresses to match the image of the man inside your head and the image you want to present to your friends and family

This cult-like indoctrination isn't, nor has it ever been, or will ever be, about love. You can continue to lie to yourself all you want to, but this form of control is about your selfish desires of wanting a specific type of man and the psychological pain of not wanting to be alone.

This state of mind subsequently forces you to make the most egotistical decision possible: become a puppet master who intends to control every aspect of your relationship.

Men are not dogs. You cannot buy their undying love and loyalty. Your sexual erotic treats may hypnotize men for a season, where they'll enthusiastically grant you the elaborate, romantic desires of your heart that you've requested. However, their financial generosity isn't anything but transactional, sex for monetary gifts.

What you believe and have been gladly proclaiming as true love and loyalty from your lovers may be the modified actions of men whose behaviors are in response to the sexual treats you have given them, the acts of romantic predatory men indulging in your control games to obtain what they truly want and desire—sexual pleasures by any means necessary. Have you ever heard the phrase, "Game recognizes game?" It means that players, like romantic predatory men, are conscious of being played.

Well-intentioned men who envision you as their wives will gladly give you the gift of their hearts. They'll find themselves compelled, as ordained by a higher power, to forsake all others and follow their hearts into becoming one with the woman they love. You should ask yourself, why do you keep playing the same manipulative control games when you see all your relationships have failed?

Don't get me wrong; many have profited sexually, financially, and materially from the puppet master control games. But, as with everything else, it comes at a cost: relationships with no love, joy, or happiness; only abuse, infidelity, nights filled with loneliness and tears, and no hope of finding serenity.

Chapter 21

The Church of Fashion
and Beauty

Religions and deities manifest in various forms and ideologies and don't always conform to traditional religious characteristics. I believe everyone has a religion or a God they serve, whether they want to acknowledge it or not. Suppose you spend an enormous amount of time contemplating or are fanatically involved in what you're passionate about, like your career, politics, health, fitness, sports, food, music, the plight of cultural identity, bigotry, drug use, alcoholism, compulsive shopping, or sexual debauchery. Furthermore, if all your conversations revolve around your favorite topic, or you're trying to convert others to join you in your interest. Then, my friend, you have a religion or a deity you serve.

"Well, wait a minute, those are just my hobbies or vices; I don't believe in organized religion."

Well, I beg to differ.

Whatever you're passionate about or addicted to that inadvertently modifies your behavior and decision-making process or consumes and controls every aspect of your life, whether you believe it or not, is your religion or the God you worship and serve.

You still don't see it? Then let us look at the similarities between traditional religious individuals and what you think is your passion or hobby:

- **A religious person:** Spends most of their time in constant meditation, prayer, and worship

  You: Spend an enormous amount of your time thinking about your interests, which consumes your thoughts

- **A religious person:** Spends time reading and studying spiritual books, seeking enlightenment

  You: Spend time reading and reviewing books, magazines, or online articles, seeking knowledge about your hobbies

- **A religious person:** Gives their organization tithes and offerings

  You: Buy products and services that help you indulge in your hobbies

- **A religious person** Zealously believes and defends the values and principles of their religion and condemns those who infringe on their beliefs

  You: Zealously believe and defend your passion's values and principles, and disagree with those who infringe on your beliefs

- **A religious person:** Habitually visits their spiritual place of worship

  You: Visit your place of fanaticism habitually, whether physically or online

- **A religious person:** Constantly talks about their religion and tries to convert others

  You: Constantly discuss your hobbies and persuade others to join you

- **A religious person:** Only wants to associate with people of like mind

  You: Only want to associate with people who share your enthusiasm

Should I go on?

By now, you should realize religion doesn't have to be spiritual; even an atheist who constantly talks about their nonbelief and tries to convert others to their side is a religion unto itself.

Corporations without impunity have successfully used the philosophies of religion to reeducate, alter, and control our thought processes and behaviors as consumers. They realized a long time ago, through data analysis and statistics, that the group most responsible for their family's financial planning, budgeting, and spending was—and most likely continues to be—the women in the family.

Historically, women controlled some of the most critical aspects of family life. Their natural skill sets eventually became the foundation of the world's major industries.

Corporations also realized that men without the influence of women in their lives wouldn't shave or shower regularly and would wear the same clothing and shoes until they fell apart.

Moreover, this psychological indifference among men would most likely persist, making men unreliable consumers without a cultural change.

They also quickly realized that the financial power of families lies with those who spend and not with those who earn.

They calculated that they needed to strategically influence the spending habits of those individuals mentally and emotionally. They rightfully predicted that women, the largest and most influential block in society, would one day have the most significant sway over product development and manufacturing. Whoever could manipulate that power could become financial gods.

Taking an analytical approach to corporate marketing and examining it through religious ideologies, corporations, intentionally or unintentionally, created what I interpret as the Church of Fashion and Beauty.

I genuinely believe corporations indoctrinated society through their targeted evangelistic methodology, hidden within their product placement commercials, as they sought to gain control of every aspect of women's lives.

Oblivious to their natural skill sets ebbing away, women found themselves at liberty to worship the corporate-manufactured deity, the Goddess of Fashion and Beauty, by purchasing their products and services, and transforming their physical appearance and personality into the image of this new God. You still don't believe you have a God or religion?

Then, look at every product advertised today, and you'll soon discover most commercials are geared directly toward controlling women's image, lifestyle, and spending habits:

- The romantic gifts that women should expect and demand from their lovers or significant others
- Dating, relationships, and sex
- Hair, nails, make-up, clothing, undergarments, shoes, and accessories
- Nutrition, health, and fitness, weight loss, body contouring, and cosmetic surgeries
- Children's wants and needs
- Home and décor
- Technology

The constant bombardment of their corporate gospel within their commercial has demoralized women's self-esteem while simultaneously tantalizing and stimulating their short-term emotional desires of "I must have it" or "I can't live without it."

Unfortunately, this addictive materialistic high has led some women to feel inadequate, unloved, unwanted, or body conscious and given them a sickening fear of being alone. Demoralizing self-esteem or self-unworthiness has persuaded some women to spend what little they have or descend into substantial financial debt to quench the unbearable thirst to look like the corporate-created deity. The desire to feel beautiful at all costs, which some women believe is the only path to happiness, also leads to the forsaking of their morals and values.

Some women may even find themselves selfishly using people for financial gain under the guise of love or a relationship—walking that thin, blurred line between being in a parasitic relationship or as a hooker with her John.

Let's look at your indoctrination and participation in your new religion, the Church of Fashion and Beauty, where you obsessively watch reality shows and view social media make-up tutorials, beauty secrets, and the latest fashion trends while obsessively trying to emulate the lifestyles of Instagram models and internalizing the celebrity advice blogs claiming to know everything about how to get and keep a man loyal and committed:

- **Tithes and offerings:** You donate most of your money to your religious organization by spending it on beauty products, clothing, shoes, purses, and accessories.
- **Fellowship:** You constantly visit stores and malls, shop online, communicate, and associate with those

who are of like mind, trying to ascertain where the best bargains are.

The Image of Your Deity

Your cult-like devotion has brainwashed you into be-lieving you should do everything humanly possible to trans-form yourself into the image of your goddess of beauty be-cause your individuality and uniqueness are now entirely un-acceptable to the fashion industry's standard of beauty, and, unfortunately, your natural beauty has now become alto-gether unacceptable to you.

So, to worship and serve at this created goddess of beauty's altar, you have now given in to the following:

- Cosmetic surgeries and the regular use of undergar-ment shapewear
- The wearing of the latest fashion trends and expen-sive designer garments
- Weekly salon treatments, the ever-changing beauty products, and cosmetic tools
- Hair extensions, dyes, and acrylic nails
- The tanning or bleaching of your skin and teeth

- The altering of your characteristics to parallel your favorite celebrity idols
- The industry's dating and relationship trends and celebrity lifestyles

With the goddess image of beauty so firmly embedded in your psyche, you now only concentrate on what you believe is the most critical asset in your life: your superficial beauty. You no longer see your inward qualities as your true self, worthy of being cultivated and proudly displayed so that others will recognize your true intrinsic worth and value.

Forsaking who you genuinely are and wholeheartedly adopting the nature and attitudes of your goddess of beauty has led men to where they can no longer distinguish the difference in your physical, mental, and emotional diversities as women.

And why?

You all wear the same fashion trends and clothing, the same nails, make-up, hair colors, and weaves. Some women even surgically change their facial features and body contours to be almost unrecognizable. Sadly, most women now seem to display the same attitudes and belief structures, regardless of age, level of maturity, or lack thereof.

The Misguided Indoctrination of Men

The worship of the goddess of beauty has led men to be psychologically and physically attracted to what I call the goddess of beauty contour —an image that the industry constantly changes to maximize profitability, based on social identities, stolen cultural traits, and political expediency.

Today, it's the pretty face with plump lips, a tiny waist, large voluptuous breasts, and perfectly shaped butts that were once unacceptable characteristics in women of color.

The constant bombardment of these images in commercials, movies, social media, strip clubs, malls, or just walking down the street has led to men's misguided sexual attraction fixation. Which is the effigy of beauty you have been presenting to men, your misguided directed perception.

Benediction

I said all of this to make this one point: The beauty industry spends billions of dollars each year to evangelize its products to convince you that the only way to become beautiful, achieve self-confidence, and attract the perfect mate is to adhere to its beauty standards and principles. This false doctrine has been about one thing and one thing only: controlling your spending habits by altering your thought processes, social behaviors, values, and morals. As a result, you may have willingly given corporations the power to control your lives and relationships, where the real you — someone you haven't taken the time to embrace and love — has unfortunately become unacceptable. Your unrealistic romantic relationship delusions have impaired your vision from recognizing the indisputable reality that you've ineptly and unconsciously forborne men, including worthy men, from being attracted to the real you.

Unfortunately, your frustrations, insecurities, and fears from past relationship traumas have become repulsive. Therefore, when men ultimately meet the real you, they run away because you don't know or love the person you are.

How do you expect someone to love you when you don't love yourself?

Maybe, just maybe, it's time to walk away from this religion and take the time to discover how to love and honor yourself, warts and all.

Chapter 22

Dating Relationship Proclivities

Considering what we've discussed so far, the everyday relationship choices I've observed some women make, and the responses of men to those decisions, let's create a stereotypical dating and relationship scenario based on those realities.

Your Interpretation of a Date

You're on a romantic date with a handsome guy. Let's call him Matthew, and you believe he has promise and potential.

What's the first thing you do?

You tell him about what you're looking for in a man.

You don't discuss his qualities or value structure to vet him properly; you quickly give in to your underlying fear of chasing him away or getting the answers to questions you don't want to hear. So instead, you passionately tell him about all the romantic things you want a man to do in a relationship, wholeheartedly believing you're setting your standards:

- "Well, I want someone who'll call just to say hello."
- "Someone who'll send me flowers and gifts just because."
- "A man who'll love to take me on romantic dates or whisk me away for amorous weekend getaways."
- "Someone who'll be enthusiastic about me maintaining my appearance so I'll continue to look beautiful and sexy for him."
- "A man who'll be there for me physically and emotionally."
- "A man willing to listen and be patient and understanding."
- "A lover who can satisfy all my sexual wants and needs."

Do you realize what you've just done? And what are the potential consequences of your actions?

The falsely preached relationship doctrine of setting the standard for how you romantically want to be treated isn't a standard at all. All you did was put yourself and the potential for a great relationship up for failure by permitting your thirst to achieve your selfish romantic fantasies by empowering Matthew, whom you haven't correctly vetted, to have the keys to your heart and the road map to get between your legs. What in the hell were you thinking? And how could you be so blind as not to see your actions for what they were? —desperation! You just told Matthew what:

- To be with you, what he needs to become

- The role in the relationship he must play

- And the romantic gestures he must bestow upon you

Please let that sink in for a moment. You've now created a dating environment that will force Matthew to act out of character, altering and crippling his ability to be his true, authentic self. He may or may not possess the mental or emotional capacity to become what you want him to be.

Your premeditative actions also opened the doors to a potential romantic predator, someone who might abuse you mentally, physically, and financially.

166

The fear of vetting has obscured your vision — your so-called women's intuition — by destroying your chances of discovering Matthew's true nature and intentions. This fear, the false relationship gospel of forcing men to become what you want them to be, inevitably opens the floodgates, allowing romantic predatory men with evil intentions to walk right through the protected barricades of your heart, camouflaged as the romantic Mr. Right of your dreams.

His Interpretation of the Date

When Matthew first met you, his instinct was to form an initial impression of who you were and what kind of hypothetical relationship he might have, based on how you presented yourself and the limited conversation you shared.

He then invited you on a date, where you spent most of the time talking about yourself and what you want in a person.

Unfortunately, you did nothing to establish in his consciousness a more precise picture of who you were, which would have destroyed any possible false narratives he might have misinterpreted at your initial encounter. You chose not to allow your inward qualities, morals, and standards to represent your true beauty.

All Matthew saw standing before him was this hot, beautiful, sexual creature he may have perceived as weak and easy, a sexual being to be exploited and conquered to fulfill his fantasies. And why? Because you didn't realize it was your responsibility to guide and direct his interpretation of you, the real you, without compromise. Your unconscious yet purposeful actions ushered Matthew's intentions toward your physical beauty, so he didn't see you as a future wife.

After a few dates, he believes what he's experiencing is love, but what he's feeling is just his sexual yearnings being exploited and manipulated, which inappropriately presents itself within him as a heightened emotional sensation of gratitude connected to the bliss that flows from the satisfaction you continually gets by having your exorbitant romantic requirements met. This intimate, passionate gratitude is just the spontaneous satisfaction that originates from his natural propensity as a man to provide, which both men and women falsely interpret as love.

The Road Map

Matthew continues to follow your roadmap —the apparent path he thinks will win you over to his heart and bed — by sending you the gifts you requested.

168

"Girl, he sent you flowers and chocolates. I think you found yourself a good man; he's so into you."

"You know what? I think he's the one."

The one, the one what? What in the hell!

You told Matthew what you wanted: the flowers and the romantic weekend getaways. And now he's giving you precisely what you asked for; you think he's the one?

You don't know who this man is, and you never will, because you didn't properly talk to or vet him, yet now he's the one?

What was that word I asked you to remember?

The Game of Accountability

Let's fast forward a bit. You're now in a relationship with Matthew and living together, and a few months have passed. You're happily getting all the romance you've requested, along with financial support. As a reward for his loyalty, you've been blowing his mind sexually. You genuinely believe there's no need for him to go anywhere else because everything he desires is with you. Then the inevitable happens: he becomes tired and uninterested in the relationship and eventually stops doing everything he's been doing.

You've been patiently accepting his excuses for not fulfilling his role in the relationship. Disappointedly, you realize there's a severe problem, and all attempts at figuring things out have ended in arguments. Your frustrations have led to an emotional state where you continually point out and condemn his failures as the main factors in the relationship breakdown.

"When we first met, you sent me flowers, took me away on romantic weekend getaways, and now nothing, absolutely nothing; you've changed."

"HOW DID HE CHANGE?"

You got what you wanted in the flowers, the romantic weekend getaways, spa dates, and everything you requested. And now your relationship, which you set up for failure, seems to be at a crossroads. You now turn and blame him. You never allowed Matthew to show you who he was. You never took the time to vet him to determine his value structure correctly and whether he had any virtuous intentions toward you or just wanted sex. You jumped into a sexual relationship with him to get all the romantic things your parasitic nature wanted and longed for; that was your choice. And now that you're feeling hurt, used, abused, lost, alone, and yearning for the predictable, self-inflicted pain in your heart to go away, you've allowed your arrogance of being the victim to turn your heartache into anger, bitterness, hatred of him, and, by default, hatred of all men.

Your State of Mind

You now willfully forsake self-reflection and the analysis of your predicament and turn to your girlfriends, who are of like mind—those who have tasted the bitterness of failed relationships and would gladly allow you to wallow in self-pity.

"I thought he loved me; he used to shower me with everything I asked for; how could he do this to me?"

"Look, men are all dogs; they only want one thing, and when they get it, they treat you unkindly. They're all cheaters, habitual liars. Furthermore, if he thinks he can do this to you and walk away, he's got another thing coming; you need to make him suffer."

The Investigation

You rationalized your behavior and concluded it's not you who caused the relationship problems; either he's changed, or someone else has muddied the relationship's sanctity.

So, with your women's intuition now in place, guided by your head and not your selfish romantic heart's desires, you consciously realize the things you wanted before aren't the things you truly need.

Your newfound hunger for love, trust, honesty, compassion, faithfulness, commitment, and a vision of your future now leads you down the arduous path of discovery. You apprehensively start to contemplate the questions you should have asked and answered during the dating period of the relationship before you got sexually involved with Matthew. You now need to know the following:

- Where does he live?

- Why were all your romantic sexual encounters at hotels or your house?

- Where does he work, and what is his job title?

- Why haven't you met any of his family or friends?

- Why does his profile on social media still say single?

- Why is he still active on dating websites?

- Why does he keep introducing you as his friend?

- Why doesn't he want to attend any of your family functions?

- Why can't you reach him directly?

- Why can't you call him at his home?

- How come you only see him on specific days during the week, and why is he always conveniently unavailable on holidays?

- Does he want children?

- Does he have kids?

- Why doesn't he want you to meet any of his kids or their mothers?

- Is he still sexually involved with any of his children's mothers?

- Is he having sex with someone else?

- Why doesn't he like any of your friends?

- Why is he coming home late every night now?

- Why does he become so upset when you try to use his cell phone?

- Does he truly love you?

- Are you his girlfriend or his side chick?

- Is there a future with him as a couple or family?

- Why can't he give you a straight answer to any of your questions?

- And why do his answers reverberate as untruths?

Chapter 23

Wants and Needs

We often muddy the waters between wants and needs; if they're not clearly defined, they can easily appear in our lives as the same thing.

Wants are those inconsequential fascinations we desire; they often burn bright but quickly fade away. They never stop being beautiful or desirable; they just become ordinary. And, in most cases, we realize that the flamboyant things we crave are not as important as we thought. When freed from the fog of selfish tendencies, our perceptions allow our mental faculties to decipher that our ability to choose is often dubious. Remember that expensive dress, pair of shoes, your dream car, that hot guy or beautiful girl you wanted? Where are they now? Probably somewhere in your closet, given away, dumped, or sold for new items.

Needs are fundamental requirements that sustain or enable us to live. We may want champagne, but water becomes the prerequisite to quench our thirst to survive in the heat of the day or when lost in a desert. Our need for love, kindness, compassion, and fidelity is equally crucial for our mental and emotional well-being and is just as critical as our need for water, food, clothing, and shelter.

Society has taught us that a person's physical attributes are the only things that sexually turn us on, but that's just an optical attraction stimulation. The ultimate aphrodisiac to our sex drive at both ends of the spectrum is the gratification of satisfying our wants and needs.

You may find yourself dating the man of your dreams, a doctor, lawyer, musician, sports star, actor, or model who can give you the lifestyle you genuinely believe you deserve. That prophecy of having wants fulfilled gives birth to the overwhelming pleasure that immediately stimulates your mental, emotional, and sexual construct. It also leads to surrendering your inhibitions—allowing your sexual encounters with your lover or lovers to be mind-blowing.

You may also meet a guy who truly loves you and gives you intimacy, friendship, and fidelity beyond anything you could have imagined—freeing you from the trap of being pretentious, allowing you to be your true, authentic self.

That overwhelming pleasure of your needs coming to fruition becomes the aphrodisiac to you having mind-blowing sexual intimacy.

Your Needs Kick In

Let's continue; you're still at the point in the relationship where you think Matthew has changed, yet you're unaware that your needs have started to overpower your wants. You realize all the flowers, romantic weekend getaways, and spa dates mean nothing unless you have the following:

- Love and friendship
- Trust and respect
- Fidelity and kindness
- Willingness to communicate
- Strength, protection, and a vision of your life together

However, prioritizing your wants over your needs in a relationship can trigger a distorted emotional hunger, forcing your needs to reclaim their rightful place over your desires.

That's why you feel the bitter cold of loneliness and emptiness from the lack of intimacy, the catalyst of your emotional pain, frustration, and anger amid your blissful romantic entanglement.

- You've been complaining that Matthew doesn't come home for dinner, and you're tired of making excuses about why he's never with you at family functions. But guess what?
  HE NEVER CAME HOME FOR DINNER OR SHOWED UP FOR FAMILY EVENTS; YOU DIDN'T CARE!
  You got what you wanted at the beginning of the relationship: the flowers, the romantic weekend getaways, the spa dates, the nails and hair, the shopping sprees, the mansions, the celebrity lifestyle, the cotton candy, the floating clouds, and the daffodils. Your needs didn't matter.

- You're annoyed that he doesn't listen to anything you say and doesn't value your opinions or ideas. But guess what?
  HE NEVER DID; YOU DIDN'T CARE!
  His lack of interest in your thoughts and opinions wasn't necessary because you were getting what you wanted. Your needs didn't matter.

177

- You're now arguing about the lack of intimacy and how dissatisfied you are with his sexual abilities and his blatant unwillingness to reciprocate all the sexual pleasures you've willingly bestowed upon him. But guess what?

  THERE WASN'T ANY INTIMACY, AND THE SEX WASN'T THAT GOOD; YOU DIDN'T CARE!

  You were doing all the hard work and making all the effort to please him while neglecting your sexual gratification. Your needs didn't matter.

- You now realize the way he's been treating you has been mentally, emotionally, and physically abusive. But guess what?

  HE WAS ABUSIVE FROM THE BEGINNING OF THE RELATIONSHIP; YOU DIDN'T CARE!

  You ignored all the warning signs of being insulted, shouted at, pushed, and slapped around—all because you were getting what you wanted. Your needs didn't matter.

- You didn't check to see if he was supporting his kids emotionally and financially from his past relation-ships or investing in a college fund for their future education. You weren't even concerned whether he

178

was the type of man who embraced responsibilities or ran away from accountability. But guess what? HE'S ALWAYS BEEN SELFISH AND LACKED THE MORAL COURAGE TO BE RESPONSIBLE: YOU DIDN'T CARE!

Until you got pregnant and discovered that the same apathetic way he's been treating the other mothers of his kids is the same way he's now treating you. You weren't remotely interested in whether he was financially capable of giving you the requested romantic life you wanted and taking care of his children simultaneously. You were the reason he wasn't financially supporting his other kids—you were getting what you wanted. Your needs didn't matter.

- You're now arguing and complaining he's changed and is no longer the same man you met and fell in love with, but has he changed? Or has he reverted to who he originally was after trying to be the man you requested him to be from all the fairytales, your romantic dreams, and from being your puppet on a string? But guess what? YOU NEVER TOOK THE TIME OR EVEN CARED ABOUT WHO HE WAS AS A PERSON; YOU DIDN'T CARE!

179

You weren't concerned about his morals, values, goals, or aspirations—all because you were getting what you wanted: the flowers, the romantic weekend getaways, the spa dates, the nails and hair, the shopping sprees, the mansions, the celebrity lifestyle, the cotton candy, the floating clouds, the daffodils. Your needs didn't matter; you didn't give a damn!

What was that word I asked you to remember?
Oh yeah, choice!

Chapter 24

His Revelation of Hurt

Matthew has reached a critical point in the relationship, wondering whether you're worth all his time, effort, and sacrifice. It seems like the more he gives, the more you ask, and it's never good enough. Your disregard for his feelings and constant criticism of his romantic attempts to make you happy have obliterated his self-confidence. And yet, for some strange reason, he still feels obliged to give you the desires of your heart, even though he realizes he's been getting nothing back.

So why doesn't he walk away?

Because society has continued to brainwash men into believing the inapplicable traditional relationships doctrine that a man's financial responsibility to provide for his woman is still the only acceptable way of demonstrating love.

Emotionally Drained

Although unaware he's been in a parasitic relationship where you've been sucking the life out of him, he quietly surrenders to his depression, which renders him completely emotionally drained. And, in so doing, he gives up all hope of ever pleasing you and stops trying.

He realizes you have been happy with him playing the traditional role of protector and financial provider. But suppose he mentions anything to you about you playing a more conventional position, like cooking, cleaning, better parenting, or respecting his decisions by listening, obeying, or submitting to his will—well, this sets off a nuclear bomb within the relationship. "I'm not your maid or mother. How dare you? I'm not one of those weak domesticated women from the past. Who in the hell do you think you are?"

Soul Food

What nutritional meaningfulness have you provided to feed Matthew's mental, emotional, and spiritual needs?

And please note, I didn't ask you about sex. If you're not feeding his spirit or providing nourishment for his soul, where should his recharge come from if all you're doing is depleting his resources?

Your parasitic nature has impaired you from comprehending that Matthew has been starving mentally, emotionally, and financially inside your relationship. You've been giving him sex as a treat to quench his physical needs while ignoring everything else. He now interprets your sexual efforts as a tedious household chore.

The Door and Suffering in Silence

During this period of emotional famine, Matthew finds himself mentally fatigued. His heart is now vulnerable and defenseless to the attention of other women who can quench his mental and emotional thirst, a thirst caused by the parasitic feeding that has become the catalyst, turning his suffering into resentful anger that pilots his out-of-character behavior, with little or no regard for your feelings. He's become so tired of trying to please you and being your emotional punching bag that he'd rather hang out with his friends than come home to you. His internal pain is the same emotional trauma that has forced men to suffer alone in silence because men have been taught not to whine—to grow a pair and deal with it—reinforced by those whose attitudes find the emotional displays of men unattractive.

How often has your lover come to you and complained about something you've done or raised an issue of concern that affected him? And what did you do to address his anxieties?

Probably nothing; you arrogantly shut him down by making the conversation about you and his failures and misdeeds, while blaming him for your unhappiness, which furthered his guilt, sinking him into the never-ending pit of your dissatisfaction.

Chapter 25

A Meet–Cute

One day, Matthew goes to the store and buys a cup of coffee. As the girl behind the counter attempts to give him his change, he smiles and tells her to keep it. Just as he turns to walk away, he hears what sounds like rushing water over dry, thirsty land, like crashing waves on a seashore or the gentle silence of sun rays caressing epidermis for the first time— "Thank you!"

That thank you, which stopped him dead in his tracks, was more food for his soul than he'd ever gotten from his relationship. He felt the emotional emptiness of his soul quenched, and the undiagnosed depression he didn't know he had healed. Soaring like a moth to a flame, he continues to visit the coffee shop, not for the girl or coffee but for the mental nourishment his spiritual soul needs, still unaware that this self-treatment stems from the ravenous disease caused by his parasitic relationship.

The Affair

After a while, the conversational pleasantries between him and the coffee shop girl become more; they exchange numbers, talk about their lives, and share funny moments, without conditions or expectations. Usually, when Matthew comes home, you ask him about his day, but just as an opening to start talking about what happened at your job, what you want, and what you need. And God forbid if he offers an ounce of advice—you'll angrily rip his head off and try to shove it where the sun don't shine. "Don't tell me how to fix it; I just want you to listen."

But unlike you, the girl at the coffee shop takes the time to listen to what he has to say; she seeks his counsel and appreciates the person he is. He doesn't have to pretend or walk around on eggshells because he's found the peace he's longed for in his relationship with someone else. I asked this question before, but it's pertinent here. Have you ever wondered why some of the most beautiful women in the world get cheated on or can't keep a man? As I noted, it has nothing to do with their physical beauty or how sexy they are. In most cases, it has everything to do with their partner's mental and emotional needs not being fulfilled.

So, Matthew, who's now getting his mental and emotional needs met by the coffee shop girl, naturally finds his desires amplified for a deeper, more intimate connection that leads to what eventually happens: they become sexually involved. You find out he's having an affair. And, just like any other person, you feel hurt, betrayed, and filled with overwhelming anger about his rejection of you, the realization that you've lost the dating and relationship game you were playing. You blame him for the relationship's problems and failure, but refuse to acknowledge what you did or didn't do that may have contributed to the infidelity. And why? Because you've embraced the doctrine that women are always the innocent victims in relationships, regardless of the issues, and there's no other truth that should be heard or considered.

The Storm

You feel naturally compelled to seek out the woman he cheated with to see if she's prettier or sexier than you, or what was it that he saw in her that he didn't see in you? And, if it turns out she's hotter or sexier, you become even more irritated and depressed.

187

"Oh, I see; I wasn't as hot and attractive enough for you? My breasts and my butt weren't voluptuous enough."

You then accuse the coffee shop girl of being a dirty slut, trying to steal your man because there's no other rationale for why he'd consider leaving you, other than her just being a cheap piece of ass. And God forbid if she's not as beautiful or as sexy as you are.

"Her? You slept with her? Of all the other women you could have slept with, you had sex with her? Oh, I see; you got that bitch to do all the nasty, dirty porn star things I wouldn't let you do to me. Her—you slept with her."

The Agony of Disaster

The relationship ends, and you're hurt, angry, and bitter, but you still don't understand or want to comprehend that you're the one who set the wheels of failure in motion, leading to your relationship's demise.

- You went after your wants; you didn't care about your needs. You orchestrated the role you wanted him to play and outlined all his romantic obligations.

- You tricked yourself and him into believing the romance he was showering on you was love.

- You turned a blind eye to all the things you should have seen as red flags at the beginning of the relationship.

- You chose not to properly vet him, to understand his value structure and his beliefs in associating sex with love, sex with fidelity, and sex with commitment.

- You loved the idea of love, but it became all about your desperation to avoid being alone.

- You bought into the false gospel that your relationship was about you, how beautiful and sexy you are, and that your inward qualities did not matter.

- He never knew you; he only met your representative, not the real you.

- You never fed his mental and emotional needs; you thought all he needed was sex.

- You used sex as a treat to get what you wanted.

- You never loved him because you couldn't; you didn't love yourself.

- You didn't see that you were a relationship parasite draining his resources and leaving him vulnerable to the attention of other women. It was all about control.

Chapter 26

Value and Self-Worth

Throughout our discussion, we've discovered that women's self-worth in the past was often derived from the skills and morals their families passed down from one generation to the next. These gifts gave women confidence in knowing who they were and their social position in their families and communities. I want to connect a few more dots on this issue.

Dowry and The Bride Price

"The money, goods, or estate that a woman brings to her husband in marriage" ("Dowry," n.d.).

According to Theodore Karasavvas (2019), "A dowry is meant to be a type of financial security in widowhood or against a neglectful husband and can also ensure economic independence for children. The dowry given to the groom is then gifted back to the bride, which remains under her ownership and control."

"The bride price, also known as Bride Wealth, is an amount of money, property, or other forms of wealth paid to the parents of a woman for the right to marry their daughter" ("Bride Price," 2019).

The bride price didn't mean a man bought a wife like property or livestock. Families knew their daughters had worth and value. Suppose a potential male suitor wanted their daughter. In that case, he'd have to prove he was worthy of receiving such a valuable gift by replacing her with the financial equivalent of what their daughter was worth to the family. And why was this so important?

He and his family would reap the benefits of the marriage through her skill set, intelligence, morals and value structure, ability to give birth, the pleasures of her body (only for the husband), and the financial prosperity she'd bring to their new union.

Families had no intention of giving their daughters to worthless men who showed interest, but rather to those with equal or higher social standing. It had to be someone they believed would honor and protect their daughter by giving her the life she deserved. Unfortunately, this wasn't always the case; many families used their daughters' marriages to gain political power and wealth. However, even in those cases, they knew the value of their daughters.

The ideology of an independent woman is someone who doesn't need anyone financially, no one to tell her what she should do, or whom she should date, or have sexual intercourse with. Regrettably, some women have disregarded the value and self-worth their family would have given them and replaced it with a false self-esteem evaluation of their physical and sexual desirability, not rooted in reality. This unrealistic view has allowed some women to think more highly of themselves than they should.

I know what I just said goes against everything society preaches today about self-esteem, how men need to accept women for who they are, and that women shouldn't settle for anything less than what they believe they deserve.

However, this irrationally adopted mindset, spawned by the delusional evaluation of desirability, has allowed some women to blindly give themselves away sexually to unworthy men with irresponsible habits and commitment phobias. It has also led to the fallacy of thinking you deserve only to date men from the higher echelons of society.

Dating and Relationship Market Value

Through directed perception, you determine and present your values and self-worth to the world; in other words, you control the marketing of yourself through your actions and given image, regardless of whether that picture is truthful or not.

Your dating market value isn't calculated based on how beautiful, sexy, or desirable you believe you are. Neither is it based on your career, your businesses, or the numerous compliments you frequently receive.

The consumers of beauty and sex appeal are the ones who calculate and determine the market value of women's desirability in dating relationships. Those consumers, believe it or not, are men who'll choose unilaterally what a woman's importance is to them.

You may not like it or want to accept it based on your own misguided opinions, but this is the absolute gospel truth for dating and relationships.

A product's value to the customer is determined by the market, not the product itself; the market dictates its price based on consumer demand. If no one wants that product, it will sit on the shelf, expire, or the company that produced it will stop manufacturing it.

Your internal and superficial beauty is the product men consume, and, as I said earlier, once a man determines your value to him, it won't change, no matter how exceptional you think you are.

Suppose most of the men you've been dating have treated you as one-night stands, friends with benefits, side chicks, or placement holders, and none of them have committed to you in the fellowship of marriage. In that case, your dating/relationship market value to men may be nothing more than sexual.

The Desires of Men

There's no secret organization of men actively researching how to tear down women's self-esteem; you do a great job of that all on your own through the criticism of other women's anatomies, appearance, and socioeconomic status.

Men who are sexually interested in you don't give a damn about your hair, nails, make-up, designer clothing, or shoes. They only care about the superficial pleasures they get from observing what they consider your most desirable physical attributes: your breasts, your legs, your hips, and your voluptuous butts, which are the visual stimuli that turn men on sexually. And, yes, men are fascinated by how you present those physical attributes to them.

Please listen carefully, for there's something about men you need to know and accept as an established truth. And it's not sexist in any way, shape, or form. You are and will always be the object of men's desires. You may choose not to accept this concept as fact, but it won't change how men have felt about women since the dawn of time. Past kings and political leaders' foolish, lustful desire for women brought their kingdoms and dynasties to their knees. That's why I've consistently stated the importance of you being responsible for guiding men beyond your physical appearance.

You also need to understand that most men don't care about your feeble attempts at physical perfection. Only you and your girlfriends care about that crap: the preponderance of men don't.

- You could have one leg and one arm, and some men will still find you sexy and desirable.

- You could have a hot, sexy body and be as ugly as sin, even missing all your teeth, and some men will still find you sexy and desirable.

- You could have a freckled face, small breasts, and no butt, and some men will still find you sexy and desirable.

- You could have fantastic legs and be as old as the hills, and some men would still find you sexy and desirable.

- You could be disabled and unable to speak, hear or see, and some men will still find you sexy and desirable.

- You could have a nasty, stinking, messed-up attitude, and some men will still find you sexy and desirable.

- You could be poor, have no job, live at home with your parents, and be as dumb as a bucket of rocks, and some men will still find you sexy and desirable.

- You could be crazy as hell, need medication, or need to be institutionalized, and some men will still find you sexy and desirable.

- You could be fat, skinny, short, or tall, and men who don't give a rat's ass will still find you sexy and desirable.

And why? Because everything men do in this life is based on their desire for you.

Men have an enormous appetite for women's vast array of physical attributes. The problem is that men's natural desires have become entirely unacceptable to you.

You have allowed the beauty industry's false gospel to brainwash you into accepting one standard of beauty for all women, which has coerced men into only desiring women who possess the attributes of the goddess of beauty, whether natural or purchased.

This misguided transformation in women has led men astray from mentally and emotionally selecting inner qualities as the genuinely unique, erotic exquisiteness of women. Regrettably, women have become increasingly enraged and disappointed at the very thought that men no longer seem to want their natural aesthetic appearance.

Symptoms of Self-Hate

Here's another natural detail you need to acknowledge about men.

When a man is in a relationship with you, it doesn't mean he stops or turns off his natural proclivities to find other women and their physical attributes beautiful and desirable.

You may not realize it, but you deliberately allow your dysphoric body-conscious issues to affect your comportment. Suppose your date or boyfriend looks or glances at another woman who may be prettier, have bigger breasts, or have a better-looking figure. In that case, the sentiment of "I'm not good enough" causes you to become highly offended, disrespected, and immensely angry at the thought that your partner may desire someone more physically attractive than you.

Who told you it's your right to force men to stop finding other women attractive when they're in a relationship with you?

Your partner's instinct to consider different women attractive has nothing to do with their love, fidelity, or your charge of disrespect. You have allowed your insecurities to place this burden on men to ease your self-hate, emotional pain, and damage.

Your lack of self-confidence has also led you to care more about what you believe other women think or say about you rather than what you think or feel about yourself. And, unfortunately, you no longer dress to impress men; you now dress to immerse yourself in the admiration of other women you don't even know.

Chapter 27

Lost Identity

I have highlighted earlier significant historical occurrences that contribute to how women view themselves today. Modern women, especially women of color, still suffer from the lingering effects of those same factors passed down from generation to generation, creating an inferiority complex of self-hate.

In earlier discussions, I theorized that the beauty industry manipulated and perpetuated self-hate by creating an unrealistic standard of beauty that has instituted a twisted culture of identity loss. Some women no longer see themselves as unique, naturally attractive, and part of the vast spectrum of feminine beauty, worthy of love, honor, and respect.

Unfortunately, some doors we open in our lives may dismayingly close, leaving nothing but painful scars that will affect our relationships and futures.

According to Rockoff (2004), the National Bureau of Economic Research, "When the war began (World War 1), the U.S. economy was in recession. But a 44-month economic boom ensued from 1914 to 1918, first as Europeans began purchasing U.S. goods for the war and later as the United States joined the battle."

This unfortunate reality of war gave companies the economic changes they needed to maximize manufacturing while simultaneously fighting the social changes of accepting that women can do the same jobs as men at war and want equal compensation. This economic and social change, driven by force, allowed certain women, who weren't a significant part of the labor force, to leave their traditional roles as stay-at-home wives and enter the industrial workforce.

Notwithstanding, it would seem indifferent not to acknowledge the history of Black female labor in America. After the Emancipation Act (National Archives and Records Administration, 1863), formerly enslaved Black men's compensation for work was far less than what they had financially generated as enslaved individuals. This lack of sustainable financial wages forced formerly enslaved Black women and their children to enter the newly paid workforce. Unfortunately, Black women, who've always been a major low-wage part of the labor force in this country, had none of the luxuries of White working women, who were a tiny minority. Social and political racism and discriminatory practices meant that Black women were considered only good enough for domestic jobs; even Black girls as young as nine were laundry workers.

According to Goldin (1977), "Although white women have only recently entered the workforce, their black counterparts have participated throughout American history."

The makeup of the working female labor force in 1880 by race and marital status for Southern cities was as follows:

- 73.3 percent of single Black women worked compared to only 23.8 percent of single White women. And when those White women got married, they left the labor force.

- 35.4 percent of married Black women worked compared to only 7.3 percent of married White women.

The word "domestic" carried a negative connotation in Southern White society, which deemed other White women who couldn't afford housemaids equal to enslaved women. Even today, the term domestic is used with the same negative connotation and spoken of in feminist circles as a form of female slavery by men and as masculine toxicity against women. Let me pause for a moment and address this issue of toxicity. From slavery to the Civil War, emancipation, reconstruction, Jim Crow laws, segregation, and race riots, the standard set by White society was that men were supposed to be able to give their women the financial luxury of being homemakers, contrary to what feminist groups today would have you believe. White women were proud of being homemakers; having someone else do their domestic chores was a badge of honor.

Black men carried unseen pain, embarrassment, and belittlement for generations because they couldn't financially provide their mothers and the women they loved with the same luxury as White men did for their wives. And there was a burning anger at knowing their wives had no choice but to clean other people's homes, take care of other people's children, and prepare other people's meals while, at the same time, knowing their wages (as Black men) were not enough to survive in a world that treated them as less than dogs. That unseen burden of Black men still reverberates in their lives today as one of the many emotional scars Black men hide.

Unfortunately, some women of color parrot that same false feminist rhetoric of female domestication. However, this feminist charge against Black men is far from the truth and is simply toxic misandry.

- Black men want Black women to be subservient.

- Black men are intimidated by successful, assertive Black women.

- Black men don't protect Black women.

- Black men ain't "Sugar–Honey–Ice–Tea." (Shit)

Regrettably, today's modern women spend their entire lives trying to conform to someone else's standards of beauty while abandoning their moral principles.

Furthermore, for women of color, the degradation of their physical attributes, beauty, and skill set goes further back. Their physical attributes, once considered substandard, are now the same physical attributes that companies promote as the new standard of beauty. Plump lips, wide hips, and curvaceous behinds are what women of different ethnicities now intensely desire and are willing to achieve at any cost, even though the natural physical attributes of women of color are still not accepted.

Through propaganda, some groups belittled and degraded the former traditional role of women as rubbish and the subjugation of women by male supremacy. Yet, those skill sets defined the worth and value of women within their families and communities. That stolen birthright of hunter-gatherers, enslaved women, and traditional wives created and manufactured the products and services we now use today as the new standard in modern conveniences of living and education. In the past, they were the following:

- **Chefs:** They prepared or cooked all their family's meals and created many dishes that your favorite restaurant now serves as gourmet meals.

- **Daycare providers:** They cared for their own children and those of others.

- **Doctors/pharmacists:** They knew what herbs to use as natural remedies to treat their loved ones' illnesses.

Those natural healers were some of the same ones religious extremists and the church condemned as druids, shamans, witches, or witch doctors, and had burned at the stake because the power-hungry religious bigots believed healing only came from God.

- **Fashion designers and interior decorators:** They weaved or purchased materials and made their family's clothing, bags, shoes, blankets, pillows, curtains, etc.

- **Historians:** Whether male or female, the griots in the village maintained an oral or written history that they passed down from one generation to the next.

- **The nutritionists:** These were the individuals who understood the nutritional value of the plants and animals they consumed and determined their family's dietary needs.

- **Organic farmers:** Some gathered or grew their own fruits, vegetables, and hunted or raised livestock without artificial chemicals.

- **Producers and manufacturers:** They aided in storing and preserving fruits, vegetables, and smoked and salted meats.

- **Psychologists:** They ensured that everyone in their families was mentally stable and capable of fulfilling their roles. And if anyone had any issues, they could always find an elder to express their inner perturbations.

- **Teachers:** Educated their children by instilling family values and the importance of their roles.

Look, I'm not advocating you return to being domesticated homemakers—not at all. In today's modern society, no one should expect a woman to cook or clean, as that era is essentially behind us due to social advancements in economics, culture, business, religion, and politics. Women can now pursue careers that their ancestors could only dream about. However, it would help if we didn't lose sight of what we're talking about here: the manipulation of self-hate that some women experience today, which stems from their stolen identities. Fortunately, you can redefine your value and self-worth by a new standard of skill sets that, individually, you can bring to the table of a relationship and marriage.

A Deliberately Ignored Truth

Beauty and sex are not long-term determining factors regarding love, commitment, and the intimacy dynamic of men. Men are not as shallow and superficial as women think; they're attracted to and want more than just physical expressions of beauty.

A woman's education and occupational success do not intimidate most men; this perception of intimidation often justifies the behavioral changes and attitudes of successful women, who frequently adopt traditionally masculine traits. The masculine energy that emanates from women who arrogantly believe they don't need a man is what turns men off.

- Being an independent woman unambiguously means you're an adult who pays her bills and nothing more, which all women should do for themselves.

- Men want and need successful, feminine women to complement their masculine energy, not masculine traits—a concept some women haven't yet grasped.

- Being feminine doesn't mean you're weak; it's a woman's strength, superpower, and sex appeal—just like being masculine is a man's strength and sex appeal.

If a woman sees a child fall, she'll run over, pick them up, and ensure they're okay; she's operating in a feminine way. If a man sees that same child fall, he'll probably wait to see if the child gets up, dusts themselves off, and tries again; he's operating in a more masculine way.

Masculine and feminine traits complement each other in all relationships. You've always been complete as a woman, never lacking in anything or needing anyone. Your ordained feminine purpose was, and is, the divine inspiration of men, their single-mindedness, and reason to protect and serve those they love. I hope you can grasp this disregarded conceptualization that seems ripped from women's consciousness. Your relationship choices have allowed you to forsake who you are and live a life built on superficial beauty. However, it doesn't negate that your actions represent the abandonment of your feminine ministry. If you're religious-minded, God, the intelligent designer, created Eve for Adam, not Adam for Eve. Adam was the one who was found alone and lacking in the Garden of Eden. That's why I noted women are the inspiration of men. Everything masculinity created and built in this world was to make the lives of those they love easier. Look at all the unglamorous jobs men still do today that keep society's infrastructure functioning to feed their families. Do you think men do these dangerous jobs just because they want to be misogynistic?

Men have always needed you; now, you act like you don't need men. What was that word?

Choice!

Chapter 28

The Sins of Mothers

S ociety has always believed parents and elders should be highly esteemed. Although true, this societal belief has unintentionally led many daughters to accept their mother's judgments and opinions as unquestionable truths.

This undoubted loyalty leads daughters to believe that, regardless of what their mothers say or do, they still deserve their honor and respect, even if their mothers are unworthy of it. In most cases, mothers earn their daughter's honor and respect. Nevertheless, blind loyalty and trust have led daughters to be psychologically abused by mothers who've allowed themselves to wallow in the trauma of past failed relationships. Additionally, the pain of rejection from the men, whom some women foolishly chose to get pregnant by, and the burden of being responsible for children, have transformed their happy existence into a life dominated by toxicity, which they believe has robbed them of their youth and beauty. This often becomes the catalyst that determines the relationship between them and their children, if not appropriately managed. This misguided attitude has led some women to take out their frustrations and bitterness on their children, whose features or natural tendencies remind them of the hurt and pain their children's fathers caused them, as though they had requested to be born. Some mothers fail to see they're just repeating the horrible cycle of choices their mothers and their mothers before did, of not protecting themselves against unwanted, unplanned, and out-of-wedlock pregnancies.

"But what about men?"

This issue has nothing to do with men.

Daughters

Most daughters' lack of sexual knowledge stems from their mothers choosing to lie, hide, or run away from truthful conversations surrounding their past sexual exploits. The desire of mothers to be seen as righteous, without sexual sin, and not being condemned as promiscuous has eroded their willingness to pass their learned knowledge and experience on to their daughters. The lack of imparted knowledge to daughters by their mothers has left them ill-equipped to handle the psychological aspect of sex and relationships. Therefore, daughters now find themselves making the same poor choices and repeating the same devastating cycles of self-destruction, which they will most likely pass down to their daughters.

Some of the honest and intimate conversations mothers should have with their daughters regarding sex should be as follows:

- The management of their sexual encounters, romantic fantasies, expectations, and the emotional unrest of being rejected

- The pleasures of sex

- The ability to connect sex with emotional maturity

- Sexual desires and sexual appetites are behaviors often learned

- Abortion and birth control

- That sexual discipline prevents others from making decisions regarding their bodies—it's their body and their choice

- That abstinence is a choice and doesn't make them a freak
- That it's their responsibility to properly vet their potential lovers before engaging in any sexual activity
- The emotional and financial hardships they'll face as a single mother
- Their past failed relationships

Having these conversations doesn't mean you're authorizing your daughter's sex life or for them to think less of you. Nevertheless, preparing your daughter's mental faculties for life's hardships will break the cycle of kissing unworthy frogs.

Undisciplined sexual behavior and unplanned pregnancies have forced so many young women to make one of the most challenging and complex decisions—choosing to have an abortion. I've expressed this before; a decision I wouldn't wish on my worst enemy.

These are the same messages mothers should teach their young sons. As men, it will be their responsibility not to allow their sexual reproductive carelessness to put women in the position of having to make the horrible mental and emotional choice of having abortions.

I don't care if you have one-night stands, casual sex, friends-with-benefits entanglements, or what you believe is a committed relationship. If you're not legally married, you and your sexual partners should use birth control together. The question of reproductive responsibility shouldn't be an issue. Your sons, men in general, need to be taught they're also in charge of their sexual reproductive rights, and that ethical responsibility should never be in the hands of women. They also have the right to protect themselves against unwanted, unplanned, and out-of-wedlock pregnancies, and it's their bodies and their choice. The power of directed perception is not just a principle that lets men see you for who you are when looking for a mate. It's also an educational tool that helps your sons build their emotional, physical, and sexual attraction muscles, fostering a healthy, positive outlook toward women. In other words, how your sons treat women will always reflect the ethical or unethical imprints that you lay within your sons as mothers.

Your Son's First Love

When your son desires a lover, companion, or wife, what types of women do you think they'll find attractive?

213

Please let me answer that for you. The women your sons will find attractive are those whose reflections share the same value structure and inner self-worth as yours. Your son's first love is you!

Your imprint on your son's lives will lay the foundation for what type of women they'll ultimately and intuitively desire and how they'll eventually treat them.

This imprinting is the same reason you and your daughters have frail, fragile relationships. The imprint you stamped into your daughter's life reflects who you are, and her personality may unconsciously be what's so infuriating to you.

When your sons treat women with honor, dignity, and respect, it's because you laid that solid foundation within them, and you should be proud.

Likewise, if your sons treat women like whores and sluts, who do you think laid that foundation?

"Whoa, I didn't raise him to be like that."

"Yes, you did. Yes, you certainly did."

You may not want to accept this, but your son's attitudes and actions may reflect what he observed in you.

- He saw your attitude toward life, whether positive or negative.

- He saw you honoring or being untrue to your declared values and morals.

- He perceived your directed perception and how you used your physical image and sexuality as your only source of beauty.

- He saw and heard you willingly being sexually used by men, as well as your arrogance in using men for financial gain.

- He observed the unkindness, insensitivity, and exasperation you exhibited toward him because he looked like or was a constant reminder of the hostilities between you and his father.

- He saw the emotional sadness and depression on your face from the agony of allowing yourself to be physically, mentally, and emotionally abused—or the depravity and hubris from the abuse you inflicted on men.

- He internalized the unplanned, unwanted pregnancies and abortions that you and your female friends normalized.

- He heard all the regurgitation of false relationship narratives about men that you and your friends perpetuated.

- He watched his sisters play the same relationship games.

Where Have All the Good Men Gone?

Women have been asking that question for generations. My answer is simple: you haven't raised, taught, and nourished your sons' mental faculties and hearts to be good men.

How in the hell are your sons expected to see women as good or worthy of their respect, honor, love, protection, and commitment if all they see or comprehend is your deviant behavior?

"But what about his deadbeat father, who didn't step up to the plate? Aren't men supposed to teach their sons how to be men?"

What has fathers teaching sons how to be men got to do with teaching them how to be good relationship partners?

Boys raised to be soldiers in a war zone to protect their country's women, elders, and natural resources are good men, but they might not be good relationship material.

But I digress.

- Are you talking about the same man you chose to have sex with using no form of birth control?

- The same man you didn't correctly vet to ascertain whether he valued love, fidelity, sex, and commitment within his relationships.

- The same man who wasn't financially responsible, or, in the common tongue, didn't have a plate to stand on.

That man?

The man you chose to be your son's father? The responsibility of fathers has always been about teaching their sons how to protect and serve the ones they love, not whom they should be emotionally or sexually attracted to—because that's subjective. Look at your son's relationships and ask yourself the following:

- Why can't they trust or commit to the women in their lives?

- Why do they run away from unproven paternity?

- Why do they fail to connect sex with love, sex with fidelity, or sex with commitment?

217

- Why do they only see women as sexual beings to be conquered and nothing more?

That forsaken responsibility of teaching your sons to be relationship worthy was and has always been yours. Your job is to demonstrate to your sons what a good woman is supposed to be, along with all the other necessary characteristics they should find most appealing and attractive in women. You're supposed to be the standard bearers from whom women who eventually want to be in your sons' lives will be measured. Your self-worth, values, and principles; the strength of your character, skill set, inner joy, happiness, and self-love—and how you consistently present yourself to the world—are the same standards and tools your sons will use to vet and judge all their romantic interests. Unfortunately, through your actions or inactions, and by the lifestyles of the women you associated with, you promoted your physical attributes as the only defining qualities that made you attractive to men and your sons. You never saw the value and beauty in your inner characteristics that should have defined you. All your sons saw was your love and worship of your body, adorned with provocative, revealing clothing that aggrandized large breasts, voluptuous butts, and elegant legs. Therefore, your sons' sexual brainwashing has taught them to be attracted to women's compelling, desirable, superficial aspects, not their inner qualities.

So why aren't your sons attracted to good women? They don't have a referent point for associating inner qualities with attraction and sexual stimulation. And if they somehow fall in love with a good woman, they will eventually destroy the relationship through infidelity because physical and sexual attraction is all they mentally and emotionally know, just like the broken and misinformed attitudes of the men you have dated and continue to date.

Society has taught women that single motherhood doesn't have consequences. However, your sons, led only by their learned sexual desires and blinded by the fact that they haven't had instructions on how to be good relationship partners from their mothers, will be destined to repeat the same horrible sins of their fathers.

Chapter 29

The Sins of Fathers

This complex subject is one I don't take for granted. When men were hunters, they were responsible for the safety and protection of their families and their territory's natural resources.

The women who played the most crucial role in their young sons' lives imprinted the cultural importance of family values and morals, highlighting the vital role of women in their village's health, survival, and future. Those disciplined instructions laid the imperative foundation that allowed fathers to teach their sons their purpose—vouchsafing the skill sets that authorized their readiness as men prepared for their duty as hunters, warriors, future husbands, and fathers to honor and protect those they loved with their lives.

The decimation of cultures due to war, colonialism, false religious doctrine, the enslavement of people, and the modernization and disregard of gender roles within society have all aided in the deconstruction of this essential yet crucial family and community process of shepherding boys into manhood. So, when it comes to relationships, marriages, and families, men often lack a clear understanding of their purpose; they often lack self-discipline, a code of ethics, and a moral compass to guide them in their responsibilities to themselves and their families. So instead of leading, men are now led by selfish sexual desires without moral fortitude.

The reeducation of men has allowed them to aggressively cast aside their capacity to love, protect, and serve, contributing to the dilapidation of their present relationships. And because they no longer see the need to offer fidelity or marriage, this has opened the doors to the abandonment of their offspring—fatherless children now doomed to repeat the same dreadful, destructive cycles.

Daddy's Girl

One of the greatest sins of fathers isn't teaching their sons to be good men. Boys have a natural default ability to develop the qualities they need to become good men.

That road, however, will most likely be paved with hardships. And, in their wake, they'll leave behind a path filled with the shattered mental and emotional lives of the women who wanted their love and affection.

Fathers' most significant transgression or negligence is the failure to imprint within their daughter's hearts and minds an understanding of what a good man is, along with all the characteristics and qualities their daughters should find most attractive in men. A father's responsibility is to be their daughter's standard bearer, to which all men who want to be in their daughter's lives should have to measure up.

The fairytale that a good man must be romantic, always loving, kind, and never say a harsh word is a lie. True love holds others accountable.

Mothers aren't the ones who should teach their daughters about what a good man should be. The pain and bitterness from past failed relationships, or the harmful regurgitated misinformation that a man's finances and willingness to lavish materialism on women qualify him as a "good man," might skew their opinions. Fathers already know, without a doubt, what a good man is and what a good man isn't. Therefore, this knowledge should place them in the precarious position of not wanting their daughter to be used or abused through the willful misdeeds of other men.

Men know what men are capable of and all the secret games they often hide from women's view. So, fathers, who aren't misguided by romantic notions, should teach their daughters how to avoid the pitfalls of dating and relationships. However, this is not the reality in most cases; fathers aren't instructing their daughters by visually demonstrating what a good man is supposed to be. So, daughters, led by romance, physical attraction, and sexual desire, are making poor choices about whom to date, whom they sexually become involved with, whom to get pregnant by, and whom they marry. Hence, the unfortunate cycle of unplanned, unwanted, and out-of-wedlock pregnancies, the agonizing choice to have abortions, fatherless children, infidelity, financial irresponsibility, and being physically, mentally, and emotionally abused continues. Therefore, when men express their delusional dissatisfaction that they can't find a good woman, they fail to comprehend that men who choose to be absentee fathers, for whatever reason, fall short in their leadership position to raise their daughters to be good women.

Being Gay

Being gay doesn't make a son or daughter any less of a man or woman or even less of a person. Your responsibility as parents is to impart the necessary tools they'll need as individuals:

- Discipline in all aspects of their lives

- The ability to protect those they love, that is, whoever they choose to love

To disregard this responsibility is a dereliction of one's duty as a parent. Lions don't care what other lions think about their pride; they'll fight and defend their dignity and territory with their lives if needed. And to those religious parents who may struggle with this concept, Jesus said in John 13:34-35 (*New Living Translation*):

"So now I am giving you a new commandment: Love each other. Just as I have loved you, you should love each other. Your love for one another will prove to the world that you are my disciples."

This love for each other also includes your LGBTQ kids, regardless of what other people think. Suppose you believe life begins at conception, abortion is a sin, and all lives are precious and a blessing from God. Then the lives of your LGBTQ children are your blessings and shouldn't be rejected, regardless of their stated sexuality or sexual orientation. They're not a curse; you can't have it both ways.

Chapter 30

The Mommy's Boy

The concept of a mummy's boy confuses me. When I analyze women who complain a man is a mummy's boy, I hear and interpret the egos of some women wanting the opportunity to control every aspect of that man's life—demoting or removing every woman, including his mother—who may threaten the relationship she wants. Unfortunately, many women feel unprepared when entering the presence of their potential mothers-in-law.

This inferiority complex shouldn't be seen as a conflict but as an opportunity to properly vet yourself to determine whether you're worthy of that woman's son or if he's the kind of moral man you truly want. I believe insecurities, selfish ambitions, or desperation may unconsciously cloud one's judgment. So, it may force your ire to attack the moral standards of your potential boyfriend's mother, you fear, if left unchecked, will cause her son to acknowledge your flaws and conclude you are unqualified to receive his love.

Your fear of loss is why you angrily condemn your partner's mother for questioning your family's upbringing, morals, belief structure, education, aspirations, or past behavior as likely indicators or predictions of future choices.

"Well, my past shouldn't judge me; everybody makes mistakes."

Regrettably, that's not how the world works. When a person gets incarcerated for a crime, that legacy follows them throughout their life, indicating they have poor decision-making abilities and little to no regard for the consequences of their choices.

A high school or adolescent college student who posts nude photos or sends race-based or homophobic tweets—and then gets rejected by colleges or employers—can't argue against their history of poor judgment. What about convicted pedophiles or murderers? Don't their past discernments and actions matter?

If you get involved with a person in and out of jail, and six months later, they commit atrocities against you, can you use the argument or excuse that their past didn't matter?

You blatantly ignore that mothers who raised their sons to be good men want the women who date or marry their sons to be of good quality. You fail to comprehend that mothers possess the same inclinations as all other women. They've been there and have done that, and aren't blind to the cunning romantic gestures women make toward their sons. They can see right through their son's relationship noise and recognize the dating games some women play by using feminine enchantments to abuse and entrap their sons into a life that will be heartbreakingly toxic. Therefore, there's nothing wrong or offensive about being vetted by a guy's mother to establish who you are. What good mother wouldn't question your intentions toward her son by examining the following:

- Your history of poor choices in men
- Why did none of the men you dated, including your children's fathers, choose not to commit to you
- Your past sexual etiquette

Her vetting gives her a window into your soul, where your past and present convictions determine whether you're a relationship parasite—who will drain her son's life, emotionally and financially—or whether your current demonstrative manifestations will be a blessing in his life. Once her vetting has proven you worthy, you'll most likely have a strong ally in your relationship with her son.

This process is the same method good fathers use to vet men interested in their daughters. Isn't this what women have been fighting for in society, to be equal? Then being vetted by a guy's mother is the price of true equality of the sexes. Here's another question on equality: why should a man want a woman who still lives at home with her parents?

I'm convinced some women like men who live alone because it allows them to have the adult relationship they want—an environment they can control, with no one looking over their shoulders and questioning their actions, a place they can move into and have a family of their own. However, a man living on his own doesn't necessarily mean he's a responsible individual or wants a live-in girlfriend or children. Some women often discover their nesting game doesn't always work out the way they want because their boyfriend's house is his sexual lair.

Have you ever considered that the guy who still lives at home with his parents may be saving his money to buy a home or start his own business, or he may be financially helping his parents rather than paying rent to someone else? His reverence toward his parents as a financially responsible son may be his way of showing them honor and respect for everything they've done. Maybe that's one of the qualities you should find most attractive in a man. And why? Because that same level of financial discipline he's been displaying throughout his life is the same quality he'll honor you within a relationship or marriage. Perhaps, instead of negatively perceiving men as mummy's boys, you should start viewing them as having the qualities needed to be good men their mothers have been protecting from romantic, predatory women. Maybe you should ask yourself, are you one of those romantic predatory women?

A Mother's Lost Soul

On the other side, some mothers have felt the weight of being habitually used and rejected by the men they once loved, and they've found themselves trapped in a sea of perpetual distress, where they're psychologically incapable of steering their emotional ship to port. They unconsciously start to see their sons as the only men who have ever loved them unconditionally and will never abandon them or fail to give them the affection they need. This psychological transference of emotional attachment unconsciously allows mothers to raise their sons as carbon copies of the men they desperately want. However, this transference isn't sexual in any way; it's simply the emotional high that comes from having a physical connection with someone who fulfills their emotional needs by giving them a sense of purpose, joy, happiness, and love. This transfer of affection is why some mothers view other female interest toward their sons as an assault or an enemy combatant who needs to be destroyed, without mercy. You then misinterpret your potential partner's mother's extreme vetting as uncalled for, strange, and weird. Yet, unintentionally, you failed to realize you're asking this woman, his mother, to relinquish the only safe, reliable person and relationship with unconditional love she's ever known. Who in the hell do you think you are that she should abandon her son's love and affection for a woman she doesn't know and doesn't trust? You might be a wolf in sheep's clothing, coming to do the same harm that was done to her by his father to her son.

Your initial response is to rush in and fight rather than understanding the environmental dynamics you want to be part of; regrettably, her son isn't the only relationship you must forge. You need to earn his mother's trust and respect as an ally in her son's happiness. In time, along with his assertiveness, she'll learn to let go, granting you your rightful place as his new queen.

"The Queen is dead, long live the Queen."

Chapter 31

The True Queen King

We all shoulder specific responsibilities—whether we accept them is our choice. However, not acknowledging them doesn't negate the fact that they still exist, and all our decisions, or indecisions, still have consequences.

The lion is the king of his pride, but his role is servitude. His job is to protect his family and territory at all costs, charging into battle with no regard for his safety or life, except for the preservation of his pride.

The matriarch lioness, the respected mother of her pride, is the true ruler. She's the unwavering and ultimate Queen King.

- She leads the hunts.

- She lays down the law by keeping everyone in check.

- She ensures her protector, her king, is well-fed in all aspects of his life so he can defend their pride land.

- She trains the members of her pride by passing on the knowledge and skill set needed for their survival.

- She, along with the other lionesses, gives birth to the next generation, ensuring the continued life of her pride and species.

- She builds the common bonds of love, respect, and unity that keep the pride together as a family unit.

- She helps maintain and protect the balance of nature by killing off the sick and weak prey animals.

A queen is chosen or inherits her throne, so she doesn't have to be ambiguous about her position or who she is. She knows her role and is proud to administer her responsibility to the best of her ability. And if anyone forgets or disputes her position as queen, she has the right to remind them with an iron fist.

Having a defined role doesn't mean your life is less important; sometimes, it's just naturally based on your abilities, which leads to the positions you play for the benefit of your family. Your role in your marriage doesn't have to be cooking, cleaning, or taking care of the kids; if you have a college degree, a profession, or a skill set that allows you to make the most of the finances in your family, then that's the role you should play. And it shouldn't make your partner's life feel insignificant. For generations, men were the bread-winners or made more money than women, based on available jobs, but that never stopped men from being with women who made little or had no jobs. Men had no problem with dating down, unlike many women today. Suppose your boyfriend or husband's role in your relationship creates an environment where you can earn the majority of the necessary income, bringing home the bacon. In that case, he's playing his role as a leader and provider in your family. The lion's job isn't just to protect his family from danger; it's to defend his territory so his family can have the essential resources they need to thrive. His protection of the pride land and the food resources gives the lionesses the freedom to hunt and provide.

You should never be ashamed of or belittle the roles you or your partner play within your relationship or marriage—or allow others to do the same. And, truthfully, based on equality, you should have no defined role for each other. You both should do whatever it takes to make your union work 100% on both sides. If you're not a man's legal wife, let him wash, cook, and clean his house. In the same way, if he's not your husband, he shouldn't be forced to help you pay your bills or take care of your other financial needs; you should be financially responsible for yourself.

Becoming Queen

Before a princess becomes queen, her servants instruct her in her duties, ensuring she's well-prepared to take her rightful place as the new queen. Unfortunately, to become the new queen, the old queen must die.

If you're in a common-law relationship, married, or live on your own, you're the queen of your kingdom, and, like in any other realm, there can only be one living and ruling queen.

When a new queen enters a room, she's no longer told what to do; her servants, who were once her teachers, wait patiently for her commands and directions.

Your mother or mother-in-law should have no say in your household; you're no longer a princess who needs instruction.

This rule also applies to single women who live independently; they've taken up the mantle of queenship, and, therefore, they've become their mother's equal, a concept many women have failed to grasp.

Unaccepted queenship has perplexed and angered many daughters and wives for generations by creating an inferiority complex that allowed them to be bullied and belittled by their mothers and mothers-in-law concerning how they dress, cook, clean, decorate, and care for their husbands and children. They've often felt woefully inadequate in living the life their mothers or mothers-in-law want them to live. Eventually, this burden manifests in their relationships as constant arguments with their partners. If you don't accept that you're your mother's or mother-in-law's equal, their opinion of you will rule over your life forever. You cannot live your life in servitude to another queen; a queen doesn't allow another queen to dictate her life. Your independence has nothing to do with you not honoring and respecting them and their opinions; they're not respecting you as a sovereign queen. Your husband needs to be aware of your feelings and not any of that nonsensical crap he should know. He's your protector, so let him do his job of protecting you against the enemies affecting the sanctity of your home.

Your mother or mother-in-law's criticisms should have no power over you as a queen; you're not their punching bag. Their opinions about your home and marriage should be shared only upon your request, not volunteered.

"Long live the queen."

Chapter 32

The Church Girl

For as long as I can remember, the message preached to single women in the Church was that all they had to do was pray and believe, and God would send them the husband they desired. But nowhere in the Bible does that scripture exist, nor does any other scripture declare such a doctrine. The Scriptures, however, indicate that having faith and doing the work are the only proven methods to achieve success.

"In the same way, faith by itself, if not accompanied by action, is dead" (*New International Version*, James 2:17).

Unfortunately, what makes this situation even worse is that the older married women in the Church, who should encourage the younger women to reach for the stars, pursue their degrees, be financially responsible, and set standards for themselves, are often the same ones who are most critical and judgmental.

In their quest to be holy and righteous, older church women have become so spiritually minded that they've forgotten how to be earthly good.

None of their past transgressions, like fornication, having kids out of wedlock, or having abortions, are considered when they pass judgment and condemnation on the younger women in their congregations.

- "All your girlfriends are getting married; why aren't you?"
- "Your eggs are getting old; don't you want kids?"
- "Are you gay?"
- "How do you expect to find a man if it's just about your career?"
- "Look at the way you dress; how is that holy?"
- "The guys you date must be men of God; being unequally yoked is unacceptable."

Equally and Unequally Yoked

Being equally yoked has been interpreted by the Church to mean both individuals must have the same faith and even belong to the same religious organization.

"Do not be yoked together with unbelievers. For what do righteousness and wickedness have in common? Or what fellowship can light have with darkness? What harmony is there between Christ and Belial? Or what does a believer have in common with an unbeliever? What agreement is there between the temple of God and idols? For we are the temple of the living God" (*New International Version*, 2 Corinthians 6:14-15).

However, nowhere in that scripture does it mention marriage or relationships. It was commenting on idol worship. The Church, however, infers that it does, and past experiences with religious relationships have shown us that people in relationships involving different faiths or non-belief structures sometimes don't work.

Notwithstanding, Paul the Apostle also wrote this about married couples:

"If the husband or wife who isn't a believer insists on leaving, let them go. In such cases, the believing husband or wife is no longer bound to the other, for God has called you to live in peace. Don't you, as wives, realize that your husbands might be saved because of you? And don't you husbands realize that your wives might be saved because of you?" (*New Living Translation*, 1 Corinthians 7:15-16).

Did this scripture explicitly declare that there's an off-ramp for spiritually unequally yoked married couples? Yes, it does, and that off-ramp is called divorce.

The scripture, 2 Corinthians 6:14-15, states, "How can a Christian be a partner with one who doesn't believe?" But what does one who doesn't believe mean?

- Are we talking about those who don't believe in God?

- Or are we talking about those who confessed to believing in Christ and attending Church every Saturday or Sunday, but their lives and actions aren't rooted in God's principles? Are we talking about those unbelievers?

The misinterpretation of being equally yoked has led many religious women and men to be trapped in loveless, unhappy, abusive marriages because they believe divorce is a sin and that staying married is the will of God. However, what scriptural justification has led you to believe God ordained your marriage in the first place?

- Maybe you got married because you gave in to your mother's nagging to give her grandchildren.

- How do you know your marriage wasn't about your partner's selfish, materialistic sexual desires or your own?

- How do you know your husband or wife didn't use your union to hide their true sexual identity?

- Or maybe the guilt of fornication pushed you or your partner into marriage.

How does being spiritually yoked justify that you have nothing in common with your partner? And when has that ever worked out in the real world?

- Does spiritually yoked make you financially responsible?

- Does it make you less arrogant, automatically mindful, and compassionate?

- Does it stop you from lying, cheating, fornicating, committing adultery, and gossiping?

- Does it wipe away the trauma from your past failed relationships that affect your present realities?

No! It doesn't. Being equally yoked must be more than just spiritual compatibility; it must also involve all the other aspects of a healthy relationship to make it work.

Divorce

"Can two people walk together without agreeing on the same direction?" (*New Living Translation*, Amos 3:3).

What you declare and preach to the world as Christians when you stay in a loveless, abusive marriage is that physical, mental, and spiritual abuse is acceptable to you and God. And that God wants you to be slapped around, lied to, and cheated on by your unfaithful husband or wife for His honor and glory. Please describe to me, and everyone else, how God gets any credit for the pain and anguish endured in an abusive relationship or marriage.

The unproven justification used by the religious rank and file for suffering is that God is testing and purifying you. And, at the end of your great tribulations, He will pour His blessings on you like rain. Like rain? What in the fresh holy hell?

The religious argument that you shouldn't get divorced because it goes against God's will is a false narrative because marriage is not a religious convention but a civil institution regulated by governments. I know "off with my head" because this goes against your romanticized religious notion that God is the one who ordained marriage because of Adam and Eve.

241

Nonetheless, when people examine the Scriptures, they forget to account for the following:

- The cultural relevance and the historical period of the people

- The person or people who were receiving God's messages

- How the Scriptures need to adjust to the factual knowledge we have today

Stop!

I know what you're thinking— sacrilege. However, I didn't say the principles of God need to change. I noted that the stated relevance of religious scriptures, based on ancient cultural beliefs, requires amendment.

- Should we continue to believe people with a neurological disorder like epilepsy still have demonic spirits and not use modern medical science to treat their disease?

- Should women be put out of the house because they have menstrual cycles?

- Should we still stone our children to death for infractions?

Throughout the Bible, women were treated as possessions, married off as gifts and as bribes, for servitude, as enslaved people, and for the bearing of sons. Do we accept that God has no problem with women being possessions? And what about the fight for women's equality? Was it just a waste of time?

(*The Living Bible*, **Deuteronomy 22:28-29**)

"If a man rapes a girl who is not engaged and gets caught in the act, he must pay a fine to the girl's father and marry her; he may never divorce her."

Is this form of rape marriage acceptable to you? Remember, you biblically believe God spiritually ordained marriage. This romantic form of marriage was a law in the Bible.

(*The Living Bible*, **Joshua 15:15-17**)

"Then, he fought against the people living in the city of Debir (formerly Kiriath-Sepher.) Caleb said that he would give his daughter Achsah to be the wife of anyone who would go and capture Kiriath-Sepher. Othniel (son of Kenaz), Caleb's nephew, was the one who conquered it, so Achsah became Othniel's wife."

Othniel married his cousin Achsah. Is this form of incest marriage acceptable to you? Remember, you biblically believe God spiritually ordained marriage. Well, this, too, is in the Bible.

(*The Living Bible*, Judges 21:20-21)

> "They told the men of Benjamin who still needed wives to go and hide in the vineyards, and when the girls of Shiloh come out for their dances, rush out and catch them and take them home with you to be your wives!"

The tribe of Benjamin kidnapped and forced women into marriage. Is this form of kidnap-forced marriage acceptable to you? Remember, you biblically believe God spiritually ordained marriage.

(*The Living Bible*, 1 Chronicles 2:34-35)

> "Sheshan had no sons, although he had several daughters. He gave one of his daughters to be the wife of Jarha, his Egyptian servant. And they had a son whom they named Attai."

Is this form of marriage breeding acceptable to you? Remember, you biblically believe God spiritually ordained marriage.

Based on today's ethical and cultural standards of racial justice and equality, the treatment of women in biblical times was inhumane and abusive. The Church's historical romantic delusion of love-based marriages generally did not exist. According to Stephanie Coontz (2006), love-based marriage became the norm in Western Europe and North America in the seventeenth century.

Suppose your husband starts physically abusing the crap out of you, cheats on you, fathers out-of-wedlock children, and becomes mentally, emotionally, and financially undisciplined. Why should you stay married when 1 Corinthians 7:15-16 (*New Living Translation*) declares God wants His children to live in peace and harmony?

Divorce isn't a sin; it's a lie and a false doctrine that has misled many religious believers into living unhappy lives filled with pain.

Women of faith must exercise the same due diligence as their secular female counterparts by adequately vetting the characteristics of potential suitors when it comes to dating, relationships, and marriage.

The establishment of directed perception allows religious women to display their spiritual principles, informing all men that sex must and will be, as God intends it to be, a benefit of marriage.

The declaration by men that they're spiritual shouldn't be the only conclusive factor that allows church women to determine they're good men who can undoubtedly be equally yoked in the bonds of marriage.

Kindness, compassion, the ability to say sorry and offer forgiveness, respect, honor, love, and faithfulness are qualities all women, even those who consider themselves women of faith, should look for when seeking a husband.

Abortion

"Before I formed you in the womb, I knew you. Before you were born, I set you apart; I appointed you as a prophet to the nations" (*New International Version*, Jeremiah 1:5).

Here's another Scripture religious leaders used to justify their stance against abortion: the belief that God has ordained every child conceived. This scripture, however, has nothing to do with conception or abortion.

I believe the Church's and theologians' interpretation of this scripture is flawed. God wasn't talking about the Prophet Jeremiah when He said, "Before I formed you in the womb, I knew you." God was referencing the children of Israel and the coming destruction and exile into Babylon for their sins against Him. God was disappointed because He had blessed them, the remnant of the man Israel that came out of Egypt, yet they turned their backs on Him and worshiped false Gods.

Under the Old Covenant, the high priests sacrificed the sin offerings to cleanse the people. This practice foreshadowed what was to come. So when God said to Jeremiah, "Before you were born, I set you apart; I appointed you as a prophet to the nations," God was referencing that He had anointed the clans of Israel as the last high priest to all nations of the world so that, when the actual sin offering came, which was Christ, the high priest (Israel) would be ready to do their duty and sacrifice the true Lamb of God on the sacred altar, to take away the sins of men. The preparation of Israel as the last high priest was the conclusion of the priesthood ministry, which is why God treated them harshly under the Old Covenant.

I know. "Off with my head."

We'll discuss this in my next book.

"Before I formed you in the womb, I knew you. Before you were born, I set you apart; I appointed you as a prophet to the nations" (*New International Version*, Jeremiah 1:5).

- If you believe this scripture infers that God has predestined every child's conception, then this unadulterated argument must also be considered valid. If a thirteen-year-old girl gets impregnated through the brutality of rape, then we must declare that God knew and allowed her rape, along with the conception. If you accept her pregnancy as preordained by God, you must admit that God predetermined her rape.

"Before I formed you in the womb, I knew you. Before you were born, I set you apart; I appointed you as a prophet to the nations" (*NIV*, Jeremiah 1:5).

- If a young girl whose father or uncle molested her gets pregnant, doesn't that signify God knew and preordained her life of molestation, along with the pregnancy? Once again, if you accept that God ordains all conceptions, including hers, then you must admit that God predetermined her life of molestation.

"Before I formed you in the womb, I knew you. Before you were born, I set you apart; I appointed you as a prophet to the nations" (*NIV*, Jeremiah 1:5).

- When a woman gets pregnant by her boyfriend, doesn't that also signify God knew she'd get pregnant through the sinful act of fornication, and He preordained it? Then fornication must also be acceptable to God.

Are you still with me?

"Before I formed you in the womb, I knew you. Before you were born, I set you apart; I appointed you as a prophet to the nations" (*NIV*, Jeremiah 1:5).

- Suppose a husband or wife cheats on their spouse and has an out-of-marriage conception. Doesn't that signify God knew about their future acts of adultery and still predetermined their marriage?

How does this make any spiritual and earthly sense to you that God wants conception from the brutality of rape, incest, fornication, and adultery?

How does God get any glory from the tortured lives of those involved?

If this scripture, Jeremiah 1:5, or any of the other Scriptures that religious institutions use to justify the doctrine that God ordains conception—and, therefore, abortion, is a sin—then we must also conclude, based on the Scriptures, that the sinful acts of rape, molestation, fornication, and adultery that lead to pregnancies are all legitimate acts justified by God. And suppose those evil actions of men are all acceptable to God. In that case, the Church can no longer consider the actions of predatory perpetrators a sin under religious doctrines.

ONCE AGAIN, HOW DOES ANY OF THIS MAKE ANY SPIRITUAL AND EARTHLY SENSE TO YOU?

Maybe, just maybe, it's time for the Church to discuss the be-all and end-all of abortion, honestly.

Abortion Rights

Let me state this here for the record: Abortion rights have nothing to do with whether it's morally or spiritually justified. That moral or spiritual dilemma is between the individual, their conscience, and whether they believe in a deity. According to the First Amendment of the US Constitution:

- "Congress shall make no law respecting an establishment of religion, or prohibiting the free exercise thereof, or abridging the freedom of speech, or of the press; or the right of the people peaceably to assemble, and to petition the Government for a redress of grievances" (National Archives, 1789).

If you're a Christian, laws protect your freedom to practice your religion and uphold your moral values without fear. That same law also protects those who may want to practice a satanic religion and their sense of decency, and those who don't believe in religion or even a deity. No group has the right to have the government legally enforce their spiritual, moral, or secular ethics on others. We've walked down that dangerous road before, and many ethnic groups have suffered from discriminatory laws created for the advancement of others. The government's job isn't to regulate individual morality, which is subjective. Its responsibility is to pass laws establishing standards to protect liberties and rights.

One of the rights of all citizens is to have safe, regulated medical procedures, which include reproductive rights. Your moral principles or religious opinions shouldn't eclipse another person's beliefs because they don't align with yours.

I know you believe God is the beginning and the end, but everyone doesn't hold the same views; governments must allow for opposing beliefs within societal laws. Nonetheless, we tend to forget that Rome tried to wipe Christians off the Earth before Christianity was acceptable because of their opposing beliefs. Was Rome correct in doing so to protect its gods and religious and cultural philosophies?

- The principles of a religion or a group are meant for those who belong to that organization
- The laws of government are meant to govern society and protect all liberties

Those liberties include the right to have a safe medical abortion; whether it's morally or spiritually justified isn't the issue.

Sex, Church, and the Desolation of Hope

I grew up in the Church and spent my formative years in a religious school; unfortunately, churches barely mentioned sex, except in the context of sin, so young women and men learned about sex outside the Church—and rarely from their religious families. Hypocritically, young women who got pregnant were often shipped off to relatives, put out of the Church and their homes, or forced to have backstreet abortions so their religious parents and pastors could maintain the image of being holy and righteous.

Having conversations about sex or engaging in sexual intercourse isn't a sin; what the Scriptures declare immoral lies in the realm of fornication and adultery, which are sinful acts of lust and covetousness, regardless of who gets hurt.

The pressure placed on young women in the Church to find a husband pushes some women to the point that, as soon as a man walks into the Church, they automatically believe he's their future husband —the Mr. Right God has sent them. They conveniently forget about their salvation and jump into sexual relationships, hoping this will make him want to marry them as quickly as possible to avoid the reality of living in sin.

The desolation of hope of religious women waiting for God to send them a husband has also allowed some church women to squander their youth and beauty on faith and not on doing the work needed to find a husband.

They rely on scripture that states:

"The man who finds a wife finds a good thing; she is a blessing to him from the Lord" (*The Living Bible*, Proverbs

18:22) instead of trying to find a good man to be their husband.

Too often, church girls push away potential good men because they aren't the type of men their religious mothers would want them to have—the same kind of men and relationships their mothers wanted for themselves and still constantly talk about: the preacher, teacher, doctor, or lawyer. Somehow, church girls don't realize that their lack of action and their mother's mental conditioning are the driving forces keeping them single and alone. And when a guy who fits their mother's Mr. Right description comes along, they desperately do whatever it takes to become his wife, which often leads to unhappy, broken relationships and marriages that their religious pride won't let them leave. They elect to stay and suffer the pain of a broken heart in silence because they believe divorce is a sin.

Spiritual Truth

Religious people often overlook the relevant details surrounding scripture, such as the following:

- Who wrote it, when, and where?
- Who was the recipient of the message?

- What were the religious, social, political, and cultural influences of that society?

- What role did the fulfillment of that scripture play in the New Covenant?

Many religious leaders have failed to teach that the word of God is supposed to be transcultural. That means God's principles are reflected in people's culture and the present reality of their time. You can't take messages or directions intended for the Jews under the Old Covenant and demand them from the Gentiles under the New Covenant. For example, to take a scripture based on the time when men were the dominant sex and use it in today's culture of equality would be scriptural malfeasance and sacrilege.

Allowing scripture to consider or fit into different cultures doesn't change its meaning or stop God from being God. It just means past inequalities and discriminations in the Bible must be analyzed, corrected, and put into context.

The Bible also speaks about enslaved people obeying their masters. Should we still have people of color enslaved today?

"Slaves, obey earthly masters with respect and fear, and with sincerity of heart just as you would obey Christ" (*New International Version*, Ephesians 6:5).

Monarchies in Europe and the Church have used God, religion, and culture as weapons of war to steal, rape, and enslave nations to extract their economic wealth.

The spiritual warfare the Church used against countries it invaded in the name of God forced the assimilation of the natives to serve their Christian God, along with their spiritual ways of worship and culture. This integration was all because they interpreted the native ways of life as inferior, brutal, and unholy while simultaneously stealing their lands, natural resources, precious minerals, and people.

Proverbs 18:22 (*The Living Bible*), "The man who finds a wife finds a good thing; she is a blessing to him from the Lord."

This should be rewritten, in my opinion, based on today's new cultural standards of equality and freedom.

- "The man who finds a good woman to marry, or the woman who finds a good man who desires to be her husband, has found warmth of heart, learned what goodness is, and has acquired a pleasurable and wonderful blessing from God."

Chapter 33

The Distasteful Exploits

of Men

The singularity of a man's natural inclination is companionship with the object of his desire; this predilection affects men of all sexual orientations.

You may think our discussion has only been about women's etiquette and very little concerning the dreadful deportment of men. But our entire conversations have been about men's disgraceful behavior, their abysmal lack of sexual discipline, and the moral fortitude seen through the prism of women's relationship choices. These are the demonstrative actions of women that define and grant men consent regarding what women consider permissible in their lives.

The interpretations and responses of men to women's choices are inspired and directed by the physically captivating allure of women and their moral acquiescence. More often, men have interpreted the sexual freedoms of women to mean they no longer need discipline, an ethical code, or inward qualities because they have been winning sexually. Therefore, some women often use perceived male bad behavior to define men's characteristics, which aren't internal behavioral traits but rather reactions or counteractions to the ever-changing relationship environment.

We started our discussion with the premise that it's a woman's body, her right to choose regarding health, career, and marriage, and her absolute choice to decide who gets into her bed. Centered on that, I believe it's a woman's responsibility to sexually protect herself against all romantic predatory men and all unwanted, unplanned, and out-of-wedlock pregnancies. That's why I stated it isn't men who freely run around having sex with women. It's women who are running around having sex with men, and any sexual liberties men take, other than those women authorized or granted consent for, should be recognized and accepted by society without equivocation as sexually inappropriate behavior, sexual harassment, or rape. Therefore, if the men to whom you bestowed the sexual pleasures of your bodies turn out to be dogs, liars, or cheaters, you should hold yourself accountable and shouldn't be allowed to do any psychological backflips and falsely blame the sexual dogs of war for being who they are and have always been–dogs, liars, and cheaters.

Nevertheless, let's look at what we've been discussing, including who men are and their responses to women's dating and relationship choices.

- **The facts:** Men require laws, principles, and a disciplined structure to focus their natural capabilities and aggression.

  Your choice: You pushed sexual discipline principles aside and bought into the false gospel that the only way to achieve sexual equality was to act like men. You failed to acknowledge that one of the doors that the past fight for women's sexual freedom opened allowed men to disregard their sexual discipline.

  The consequence: By default, the blatant disregard for sexual discipline created a sexual playground, which led to the sport of sex and dating. So, men, now led by their selfish, illicit desires and void of sexual discipline, are dating without any emotional attachments but with aggression and an uncompromising, animalistic killer instinct to sexually win at all costs, regardless of who gets hurt.

My inside Voice: Yet, amid this new age of sexual emancipation, some women still hope today's generation of men will give them the same traditional love, fidelity, and commitment their great-grandparents had. However, modern women fail to recognize that the disregarded, former sexual discipline principles of women were far superior to the sexual ethics of men. Accordingly, when women lowered their standards to become sexually equal to men, they went from being sexually principled leaders to sexually promiscuous followers.

- **The facts:** Men are supposed to manage their sexual desires and be in command of their reproductive rights, and those rights should never foolishly be relinquished based on feelings.

  Your choice: Some women blatantly disregard self-ownership and fail to protect their reproductive rights against unwanted pregnancies through the fundamental use of birth control and the willful ignorance of not forcing their lovers to use condoms during consenting sexual encounters.

The consequence: Society's message concerning reproductive rights targeted to women has allowed men to view their sexual responsibility as a distant reality, a game of chance. They think sex isn't sex unless they can taste the true essence of a woman, flesh to flesh. So, when the sexual carelessness of men and the imbecilic sexual choices of women collide, and pregnancy manifests itself, some men's undisciplined, moronic immaturity causes them to run away from responsibility, just like the little boys they genuinely are.

My inside voice: Irresponsibility has become the brand of men that some women keep allowing themselves to be sexually attracted to, which appropriate vetting would have ruled unqualified. Yet these same careless men have multiple children and will continue to breed irresponsible women like cattle. Unfortunately, women will still have to deal with the emotional burden and guilt regarding their poor choices and the harsh reality of raising children alone with no financial or emotional support, and navigating the bitter option of having abortions.

• **The facts:** Moral principles are no longer considered a sexy or attractive quality in men to some women.

261

Your choice: Some women have allowed their emotional and sexual desires to develop an appetite for only sexually experienced partners, men with status and wealth, while completely ignoring all the other inner qualities needed for a healthy relationship and future marriage.

The consequence: The disregard for inward qualities has contributed to the emotional delinquency of some men to disconnect sex with love, sex with fidelity, and sex with commitment in their false quest to become exceptional lovers.

My inside voice: Instead of men seeing women as their wives and the future mothers of their children, some men now see women as a one-night stand to be conquered repeatedly for their sexual pleasure.

• **The facts:** Love, fidelity, and commitment are learned and practiced principles men developed in some form of family structure.

Your choice: Some women willingly believe in the false doctrine that love, fidelity, and commitment are automatic within a relationship. Therefore, they don't seek out those qualities in potential lovers as part of their romantic relationship calculations.

The consequence: With sex given to men without preconditions, some men no longer see the need to develop internal qualities and, therefore, aren't compelled to shower women with love, honor, respect, fidelity, and commitment.

My inside voice: When men became void of inner qualities, sinful, lustful desires took root. Men became liars, cheaters, and romantic relationship predators to appease their new God—themselves.

- **The facts:** Directed perception opens the doors to self-love and recognizing your inner qualities as your true beauty and authentic self, which allows you to influence a man's interpretation of you by setting realistic, required standards. This gift enables men who consider themselves worthy of your love, joy, and happiness to approach and be vetted.

Your choice: The mismanagement of the gift of directed perception has allowed women to falsely present to men an image of who they want to be, rather than who they are.

The consequence: Some women's obsessive attempts to look like the goddess of beauty have psychologically deceived some men into no longer finding the natural beauty of women attractive.

My inside voice: Misguided, directed perception has forced men to struggle with offering women fidelity or commitment because they don't know who they could be falling in love with—those women's true selves or their representatives.

- **The facts:** Some women's unrealistic and delusional romantic requests have allowed them to ignore and reject average men, who are the majority.

  Your choice: Some women now feel that being with an average guy is settling for less, so they only seek romantic interludes with top-tier men who possess all the financial accouterments they believe they deserve.

  The consequence: Some men have forsaken their financial responsibilities to themselves, including their children, to compete in today's dating market. Unfortunately, some men don't care if their financial wealth comes from illegal activities, including the women they date.

  My inside voice: Men know financial wealth or the appearance of wealth gives them options and choices, and there's an abundance of women who will want the romantic, economic lifestyle they can provide.

These men also know they don't have to offer women fidelity or commitment; they can have as many women as they want, and, if any of those women can no longer handle their lifestyle, they move on to the next.

- **The facts:** Men's natural proclivity is to establish a mental picture of their possible associations with women. Once set, that image and reality will not change.

  Your choice: Some women's premeditated bait-and-switch games psychologically coerce men into initially being physically and emotionally attracted to their false images of beauty. Then they pivot and ask those same men to abandon those feelings and fall in love with who they are.

  The consequence: Some men, faced with the reality that the women they've been dating are just figments of their imaginations, are left with no choice but to walk away from their deceptive, insidious relationships.

  My inside voice: Some women then maliciously smear all men as dogs, liars, and cheaters because men lack the mental capacity to undertake that unrealistic metamorphosis of falling in love with who they are, a bridge most men are incapable of crossing. It seems some women have conveniently purged from their consciousness that they're the ones who led men down this duplicitous sexual attraction rabbit hole. If you don't love and accept the person you are, how are men supposed to accept and love you?

- **The facts:** Family protection allowed women to have their potential relationship partners unromantically vetted, saving them from the heartache of kissing unworthy frogs.

  Your choice: Women rejected the concept of family protection, believing it shouldn't be a part of a woman's social status as equal to men.

  The consequence: The disregard for the importance of family protection led to unaccountability from men in relationships and marriage; this allowed men to abuse women with impunity.

  My inside voice: Men are no longer enthusiastic about or don't see the need to present a vision of the future with the contemplation of marriage to women or their families because women no longer require an endgame of marriage from men.

- **The facts:** Fulfilling your wants or needs is the ultimate aphrodisiac.

Your choice: Some women ignore accountable men and run after their romantic wants instead of their needs. They make the calculated decision that they can change the men they desire into the romantic image inside their heads.

The consequence: When personal accountability comes calling, the unwanted and unplanned pregnancies, the romantic superficial qualities of the Bad Boys, Mr. Cute, or Mr. Popular become attractive, as they insinuate that you are a promiscuous liar and that the children aren't theirs.

My inside voice: The men that most women often ignore, the Mr. Boring or Mr. Financially Accountable, who is already standing on their plate with principles and morals, are the same men that some women desperately crave when faced with the reality of responsibility.

• **The facts:** A mother's responsibility is to cement within their sons' hearts and mental construct the future characteristics, values, and morals they'll find most desirable and provocative when looking for a mate.

Your choice: Some mothers have disregarded this responsibility and bought into the false premise that women can't teach their sons how to be men.

The consequence: Men are no longer attracted to women's inner qualities and splendor because they never saw those same qualities within their mothers. They now only sexually desire the superficial attributes of women because they saw their mothers, their mother's friends, and sisters making their physical appearance their priority.

My inside voice: If your sons are minimizing the value of the women they're attracted to, treating them unkindly or as one-night stands, and not worthy of their love, fidelity, and commitment. You may have imprinted that image into their psyche, so please forgive my unsympathetic utterance; you probably haven't been raising your sons to be good men.

- **The facts:** Women have the power of choice. A man's truth resides in the realm of request; that's why men traditionally ask families for permission to marry their daughters.

  Your choice: Women blatantly transferred that power of choice into the hands of men.

The consequence: With top-tier men now elevated as the prize within relationships, they can choose who to date, accept or reject, or disregard like filthy rags based on their ever-changing emotional and sexual desires.

My inside voice: True power lies in the realm of those granting requests. Men live in a realm of sub-servient relationships, where they make appeals. Some women are now desperately hurling themselves at men and giving men the ability to choose whether they want them; this isn't equality; it's stepping down to the level of men.

- **The facts:** Women judge men's value and worth based on their physique, profession, salary, wealth, or celebrity status.

  Your choice: Some women, especially those with careers or businesses, believe men should judge their value and worth using the same medium women use to evaluate men. Therefore, it should place them in the higher echelon of the female dating hierarchy, where men should desire them before all others.

  The consequence: Some women become disheartened because the men who meet their standards don't want them. These women fail to accept that men are not attracted to a woman's career or salary. Those factors are not a part of most men's romantic calculations.

My inside voice: From the dawn of time, men have chosen women based on their physical beauty, sex appeal, virtue, ability to produce children, and femininity, which are the intangible qualities that bring peace and comfort to a man's mental and emotional stability. These are men's standards, and they aren't sexist in any shape or form, as many within society want people to believe. Men, just like women, shouldn't be forced to accept anyone who doesn't meet their criteria.

• **The facts:** True equality means no defined roles in a relationship or marriage. The original concept of marriage is that couples use their skill sets and strengths to benefit their union. Marriage is not a fifty–fifty union. It's one hundred percent both ways.

Your choice: Some women believe their efforts in their relationship or marriage depend on their partner's reciprocation or that their partner or husband is supposed to have a defined gender-specific role. Yet, women shouldn't because that's not today's standard of equality.

The consequence: The denigration of men and their demotion to merely being financial providers within their relationships has led men to forsake marriage, abandon their traditional leadership roles, and relinquish their duty to protect the resources within their marriages.

My inside voice: The original idea of manhood had a defined purpose: to protect and serve those they loved. However, the false preconception of marriage roles has hindered the embracing of individual natural abilities that benefit the marriage. If your husband is better at cooking, then let him cook, as it will prevent you from poisoning him and the kids. If he's better at cleaning, nurturing, and communicating with the kids, that's the role he should play in the marriage. If you're better at fixing things around the house than he is, do it. The problem arises when we become jealous, bitter, or resentful about what we perceive as our partner's lack of effort. This turmoil can lead to issues that extend beyond being merely worked out, to issues affecting the love couples share.

- **The facts:** Some women often complain that the lack of romance in their marriage is appalling because their husbands don't buy them gifts or take them on weekend getaways.

Your choice: Women willfully ignore the maturity of intimacy within their marriages because the grass of single women's lives appears greener.

The consequence: This entertained delusion blinds women from acknowledging the actions of their partners as romance, their love language. They forget that their partners or husbands are patient and kind; the kids are healthy, well cared for, and fed; and, on weekends, they do the yard work, wash the car, check the brakes, change the oil, fill up the tank for the coming week, and pay the bills.

My inside voice: Men often suffer in silence because they're not allowed to complain about their battles and hardships in providing for their families. Their efforts get disregarded as something other than "love" or "romance." All because their partner's single girlfriends or work colleagues got flowers.

Some pillars of manhood include self-sacrifice, self-discipline, and emotional control; these qualities enable men to honor their word and commitments to themselves and their families.

Men became lackadaisical when the relationship environment shifted due to the fragility of feelings. They no longer needed to develop the inner characteristics of love, honor, fidelity, patience, kindness, and commitment.

Regrettably, the sexual gratification of men takes the lead in their relationship choices, including their reactions to women's romantic decisions. In this age of free love and sex without requirements, men have accepted that they don't have to be committed to anyone or anything to gratify their fantasies and sexual lust. This sexual playground has allowed men to become sexual gods.

Chapter 34

Wise Choices

You're probably offended that I've painted such an objectionable picture, suggesting men's distasteful exploits are related to women's dating and relationship choices. You may think I've been unfair or sexist because the directive over the years has been that men shouldn't talk about women and their shortcomings. However, the sad truth is these things are related to choices and consequences. I genuinely need help answering these questions:

- Have we gone too far and reached the point of no return in our selfish quest for sexual satisfaction and relationship dominance?

- Or have we forgotten or ignored the fundamental purpose of our romantic lives?

Our dating and relationships resolution is to find commitment, understand what marriage entails, and raise a family. We've pinned our relationship's hopes and dreams on love, an irrational principle frequently changing with our fragile emotions. We've permanently put the cart before the horse, so we've been left standing still, unsheltered and battered by the storm and chaos we've created, with nowhere to go.

I'm still hopeful, I guess, but I don't know. All the proven principles that give us what we need are the same ones we fight against through selfish actions.

- To meet our realistic requirements, uphold our ethical standards, and earn the trust and affection of those who desire us, let us make informed decisions and adhere to disciplined principles. Then our potential companions would be more inclined to self-evaluate and summon the courage to adopt those qualities that make them worthy of being our partners.

- To satisfy our needs, we rid ourselves of all delusions of romantic grandeur and choose a mate with whom we can equally build a life based on fidelity, similar financial aspirations, respect, and commitment. Our satisfaction of nccds fulfilled is what actual settling, cashing out, is supposed to be.

- Suppose we choose the path of sexual self-discipline by not casually sleeping around—that is, keeping our penises in our pants and our legs shut.

  This would force men to consider raising their basic dating and relationship standards with women beyond just being beautiful, and to contemplate choosing feminine, principled women with college degrees, careers, businesses, and ambition as the ultimate prize. Women to vet men better by desiring good men who can serve their future families as protectors and providers while disregarding romantic predators' cunning advances.

- With marriage being a prerequisite or the end game of our romantic involvements, we would stop playing dating and relationship games that have produced the disasters we see in our romantic lives. If we do that, we'll no longer find ourselves alone, burdened with unplanned children, or with nothing but the memories of past sexual encounters and conquests, and the realization that the unrealistic romantic or sexual lifestyle we wanted and longed for was delusional.

- Suppose we allow ourselves to become captivated by inner responsible attributes, the qualities we should

276

find most attractive and stimulating in a potential partner, and not just superficial characteristics. We would then reshape and refocus our spiritual, mental, and sexual attraction toward those who have consistently demonstrated attributes of love, honor, respect, and commitment throughout all aspects of their lives. Then the irresponsible individuals we once found most attractive and longed for would find themselves at the bottom of the dating and relationship totem pole, where they'll either step up and become the men and women we deserve or remain mentally adolescent fledglings.

- Suppose women acknowledge the hard truth that being a single mother is the manifestation of not mentally and spiritually protecting their life-giving, sexual reproductive privilege by allowing unworthy men to access their wombs. Women would then rid themselves of the mental anguish and chaos of considering abortions as a course correction, excluding the hardship of pregnancies caused by rape, incest, molestation, and the medical safety of the mother. Men would then have to acknowledge their irresponsible sexual behavior and disregard for their sexual reproductive rights as significant contributing factors

in unplanned, unwanted, and out-of-wedlock pregnancies, abortion, single-parent households, abandoned kids in foster care, and adoption systems.

Chapter 35

The Lost Mantle of
Power

When you rediscover your inner strength by acknowledging who you are and making wiser choices based on redefining your responsibilities and purpose within your relationships, marriages, and families, you will no longer be trampled underfoot by society's misguided notions. Then and only then will you be ready to fight and retake the mantle of power your predecessors once cast aside, which is your intelligently designed or social position as an influential moral leader. This fundamental quality becomes the inspiration or spiritual justification for the servitude of men to honor and protect those they love with their lives, to which there's no greater calling in the realm of men. The serpent in the Garden of Eden didn't go after Eve because she was the weaker vessel; he went after her because she held the power of influence. He knew Adam, who was standing with Eve at the Tree of Life, would follow her beyond the gates of death, and he did.

"When the woman saw that the fruit of the tree was good for food and pleasing to the eye, and desirable for gaining wisdom, she took some and ate it. She also gave some to her husband, who was with her, and he ate it" (*New International Version*, Genesis 3:6).

If your soul desperately yearns for true love, a relationship, and marriage, you can no longer put your wants before your needs, as you have been hopelessly undertaking.

Your journey of self-healing must begin with self-forgiveness for the lingering guilt stemming from the poor decisions you've made and the pain caused by the immoral and disgraceful acts of others against you. Your emerging self-confidence will open the portals of your heart and mind, allowing you to finally understand that your joy and happiness don't come from someone else, but from deep within your soul. Then and only then will you begin to truly see yourself as worthy of love, fidelity, and commitment. And powerful enough to command and encourage both men and women who've lost their way for generations to return to the place of principles and self-control.

The power of choice related to every aspect of your life has always been yours. Therefore, acknowledge that the romantic decisions you make will have positive or negative results.

The Consequence of Choice.

Afterword

You can't live in a bubble where the only voices you hear are repeating the same things you've been taught and led to believe. How can you learn and grow if your ideologies or accepted doctrines aren't disputed based on facts, new revelations, or scientific discoveries?

That psychological rationale is the same as a religious or secular cult that doesn't want its doctrines challenged for fear of being proven illogical.

My inside voice and conclusions may come across as harsh, arrogant, insensitive, or even mean, but my intention wasn't to offend. It was to challenge your relationship doctrine of truths learned through the misinformed verbiage of others, rather than facts.

"Well, I feel," or "I don't know, but" or "My opinion is."

These sentiments are never rooted in facts but in conclusions based on emotions.

"Every man has a right to an opinion, but no man has a right to be wrong in his facts" (Baruch, 1946).

I hope this book has led you to question and analyze everything you think you know about dating, relationships, and marriage, which may have contributed to some of the predicaments you've found yourself habitually accepting and repeating.

- Granting sexual consent without vetting
- Choosing relationships deprived of prerequisites
- Not caring whether our lovers are worthy of exclusive dating or conceiving our children
- Disregarding marriage as the endgame
- Choosing romantic wants over relationship needs
- Not including inner virtues as significant in sexual desirability
- Allowing fear to rule every aspect of romance

Suppose we course correct by embracing the forgotten principles mentioned throughout our discussion.

- Acknowledging our past relationship mistakes
- Taking time to heal
- Offering ourselves forgiveness
- Accepting that true joy, happiness, and love are internalized qualities and are designed to be shared rather than received
- Practicing and adopting the principles we will ultimately desire in others and need in our relationships

- Having a realistic comprehension of our attractiveness and relationship market value, finding our place, and understanding those who will desire us—the consumers of our exquisiteness

- Utilizing the protection of our family or tribe when vetting and dating

- Building a relationship foundation based on the principles of love and respect

- Having a vision for the future, which may include marriage and raising a family

- Accepting our responsibility to protect our reproductive rights against unplanned and unwanted pregnancies

- Financial responsibility, redefined our relationship roles, and respecting the inherent natural proclivities in each other–true equality

- Understanding that sex is not an expression of love, just one of the many benefits of relationship fidelity and commitment, and not the only form of expressing intimacy

- Marriage is the legal expression of love and protection for your family

Suppose we do these things; perhaps our time, sexual permissions, and emotional and financial investments in our relationships would not be in vain, and the gray relationship area that holds us hostage will fade into obscurity.

Mothers may, again, see the need to teach their sons the values to desire in principled women.

Likewise, fathers will teach their daughters what to expect in moral men, so our deteriorating ideology regarding relationships and marriage will diminish.

Lamentably, if all we have in our relationships is Netflix and chill, then we have nothing.

References

Ain't Nothin' Goin' on but the rent. (2023, January 7). In *Wikipedia*. https://en.wikipe-dia.org/wiki/Ain%27t_Nothin%27_Goin%27_On_but_the_Rent

Alphonse Karr. (2020, November 14). In *Wikipedia*. https://en.wikiquote.org/w/index.php?title=Alphonse_Karr&oldid=2891864

Baldwin, E. (2020). *Birds of a feather flock together*. Poem Analysis. http://poemanalysis.com/birds-of-a-feather-flock-together/

Baruch, B. (1946, October 9). Baruch upholds U.S. atom plans; Hits at Wallace. *The Galveston Daily News*, 1, 3. https://quoteinvestigator.com/category/bernard-baruch/

Bride price. (2019, June 12). In *New World Encyclopedia*. https://www.newworldencyclopedia.org/p/index.php?title=Bride_price&oldid=942786.+%28p.+188%29

Carroll, L., & Tenniel, J. (1865). *Alice in Wonderland: The Original Edition with Complete Illustrations*. Independently published.

Centers for Disease Control and Prevention. (2022, March 25). *Fast-stats—Marriage and divorce.* https://www.cdc.gov/nchs/fastats/marriage-divorce.htm

Consent. (n.d.). In the *Merriam-Webster.com dictionary.* https://www.merriam-webster.com/dictionary/consent

Coontz, S. (2006). *Marriage, a history: How love conquered marriage.* Penguin Books.

Dowry. (n.d.). In *Merriam-Webster.com.* https://www.merriam-webster.com/dictionary/dowry

Fetterolf, J., & Horowitz, J. (2020). *Worldwide optimism about the future of gender equality, even as many see advantages for men.* Pew Research Center. https://www.pewresearch.org/global/2020/04/30/worldwide-optimism-about-future-of-gender-equality-even-as-many-see-advantages-for-men/

Force. (1995). In *Cambridge English Dictionary.* https://dictionary.cambridge.org/dictionary/english/force

Goldin, C. (1977). Female labor force participation: The origin of Black and White differences, 1870 and

1880. *Journal of Economic History, 37*(1), 87–108. http://nrs.harvard.edu/urn-3:HUL.In-stRepos:2643657

Karasavvas, T. (2019, October 23). *Putting a price on marriage: The long-standing custom of dowries.* Ancient Origins. https://www.ancient-origins.net/history-ancient-traditions/putting-price-marriage-long-standing-custom-dowries-007222 (p. 200)

Library of Congress. (n.d.). *Born in Slavery: Slave Narratives from the Federal Writers' Project, 1936 to 1938.* https://www.loc.gov/collections/slave-narratives-from-the-federal-writers-project-1936-to-1938/

Marion J. Sims. (2022, October 31). In *Wikipedia.* https://en.wikipedia.org/wiki/J._Marion_Sims

Murner, T. (1512) *Don't throw the baby out with the bathwater.* (2022, October 31). In *Wikipedia.* https://en.wikipedia.org/wiki/Don%27t_throw_the_baby_out_with_the_bathwater

National Archives. (1789, March 4). *The Constitution of the United States.* https://www.archives.gov/founding-docs/constitution

National Archives and Records Administration. (1863, January 1). *The emancipation proclamation.* https://www.archives.gov/exhibits/featured-documents/emancipation-proclamation

National Archives and Records Administration. (2010, April 15). *Presidential memorandum – Hospital visitation.* https://obamawhitehouse.archives.gov/the-press-office/presidential-memorandum-hospital-visitation

New International Version. (2011). Biblica Inc. (Original work published 1973).

New Living Translation. (2015). Tyndale House Foundation (original work published 1996).

No scrubs. (2023, February 10) In *Wikipedia.* https://en.wikipedia.org/wiki/No_Scrubs

Petitioners v. Richard Hodges, Director, Ohio Department of Health et al. (2015, January 26). U.S. Court of Appeals for the Sixth Circuit. No. 14-3057, 14-3464. No. 14-556 Vide 14-562, 14-571, 14-574.

Rape. (2022, August 17). In *Encyclopedia Britannica.* https://www.britannica.com/topic/rape-crime

Rockoff, H. (2004, June 24). *Until it's over, over there: The U.S. economy in World War One.* NBER.

https://users.nber.org/~con-
fer/2005/nss05/rockoff.pdf

Santayana, G. (1905*). Life of reason: Phases of human progress.* Charles Scribner's and Sons.

The Living Bible. (1971). Tyndale House Publishers.
https://www.tyndale.com/

The writing's on the wall. (2023, February 17*). In *Wikipedia*. https://en.wikipedia.org/wiki/The_Writ-
ing%27s_on_the_Wall

United Nations Human Rights Office. (2014). *Women's
rights are human rights*.
https://www.ohchr.org/sites/default/files/Docu-
ments/Events/WHRD/WomenRightsAreHR.pdf

US Equal Employment Opportunity Commission. (1964).
*Sexual harassment is a form of sex discrimination
that violates.* https://www.eeoc.gov/sexual-harass-
ment

Wall, L. L. (2006). The medical ethics of Dr. J Marion
Sims: A fresh look at the historical record. *Journal
of Medical Ethics, 32*(6), 346–350.
https://doi.org/10.1136/jme.2005.012559

Weigel, M. (1984). *Labor of love: The invention of dating.*
Farrar, Straus, and Giroux.

Author Bio

Bernard R. Pilgrim was born in Barbados, the land of blue seas, white sands, rum, and calypso. He spent his early years in a religious school where he learned to question religious doctrines and social issues. As a talented singer, songwriter, musician, and choir director, he performed at local concerts and international festivals. This led him to music production and opening a recording studio in New York. He also owned and operated a private contracting business for several years. Despite his diverse experiences, he never expected that his skills in creating corporate documents, composing music, and writing song lyrics would lead him to literary work. However, his keen observations of romantic relationship behaviors and numerous conversations with family, friends, and acquaintances have given him unique insights into the complexities of modern relationships. These insights inspired his first book, "The Consequence of Choice: My Inside Voice."

The House That Independent Publishing Built

www.soursoppress.com